TAKE
CONTROL OF
ADHD

TAKE CONTROL OF ADHD

The Ultimate Guide for Teens With ADHD

Ruth Spodak, Ph.D.
and Kenneth Stefano, Psy.D.

PRUFROCK PRESS INC.
WACO, TEXAS

Library of Congress Cataloging-in-Publication Data

Spodak, Ruth, 1942-
Take control of ADHD : the ultimate guide for teens with attention problems / Ruth Spodak and Kenneth Stefano.
    p. cm.
Includes bibliographical references.
ISBN 978-1-59363-535-0 (pbk.)
1. Attention-deficit disorder in adolescence--Popular works. I. Stefano, Kenneth, 1964- II. Title.
RJ506.H9S6595 2011
618.92'8589--dc22
                            2010051380

Edited by Lacy Compton

Cover and Layout Design by Marjorie Parker

ISBN-13: 978-1-59363-535-0

Prufrock Press Inc.
P.O. Box 8813
Waco, TX 76714-8813
Phone: (800) 998-2208
Fax: (800) 240-0333
http://www.prufrock.com

DEDICATION

To my sons, Doug and Jeff, and their wonderful wives and children—continued sources of love and joy.

—Ruth B. Spodak

To Mike and all of the other boys and girls with ADHD who have worked with me over the years. Your stories have touched me and your successes have inspired me. You are the reason that I do what I do.

—Kenneth Stefano

CONTENTS

Chapter 1

Chapter 2

Chapter 3

Chapter 4

Chapter 5

Chapter 6

Chapter 7

Chapter 8

Chapter 9

Your Attention Profile

ACKNOWLEDGMENTS

There are many people we would like to acknowledge for their help and support with this project. Dr. Larry Silver, one of the major authorities in the field of Attention Deficit/Hyperactivity Disorders and learning disabilities, has been a source of inspiration and support throughout our professional careers. We are grateful that he continues to be someone we can turn to for advice with complex diagnoses. We also want to thank Rich Weinfeld who, by example and encouragement, started us on the track of writing this book.

We thank our editor, Lacy Compton, who has answered our multiple questions and been a source of support as we worked through this process.

On a daily basis, Margaret Ascienzo, who technically is our Office Manager/Intake Coordinator, but is really the glue that holds our office together, provides us with the support and structure we need to be effective. A very special and heartfelt thanks for her enthusiasm, her warm and welcoming attitude to parents and students, and for always being there for us and the rest of our staff. We don't know how you carved out all those blocks of time for us to work on this book, but we really appreciate it.

We are grateful to our friends and colleagues who have read this book and provided us valuable feedback and suggestions.

A special thank you to all of the students with ADHD who let us interview them for this book. Your stories and quotes were honest, insightful, and oftentimes humorous. A very special acknowledgment and thank you to all of the students with ADHD we have worked with over many years. Your confidence in us, your hard work, and the successes you have experienced have provided us with the inspiration to continue in this rewarding profession.

FOREWORD

have read many books on ADHD that were written for adolescents. Each has useful information. Each educates the reader. It was with this expectation that I read *Take Control of ADHD: The Ultimate Guide for Teens With ADHD*. I quickly realized that this book was different.

If I were a teen reading this book, I would feel like I was sitting in a room with two caring individuals who understood me, knew my struggles, and wanted to help. I'd feel as though the authors were looking directly at me and speaking directly to me. Ruth Spodak and Ken Stefano have succeeded in using a style of communication that is both informative and personal. The reader senses that the authors understand and that they want to help. The authors provide useful and practical information. They then use this information to empower teens to take control of their lives and to take action.

The first four chapters provide the information needed for the teen to understand who he or she is as an adolescent with

ADHD. Chapter 1 explains what ADHD is. Chapter 2 discusses the possible causes of ADHD. Chapter 3 illustrates the types of ADHD and what behaviors go with each type. Chapter 4 gives a realistic view of how long ADHD might last.

Chapters 5 through 8 discuss what the teen can do. He must join with his parents and school professionals to work on the consequences of having ADHD. The information provided empowers the teen to take ownership and to take charge of his or her life. Chapter 5 explains the role of medications. Chapter 6 explains how the teen can get help with schoolwork. He or she learns the forms of individual help available as well as the types of accommodations that might help with ADHD. Chapter 7 explains the classroom teacher's role, stressing how the teen needs to work with his or her teacher and other school professionals. Chapter 8 discusses four different areas where teens with ADHD can advocate for and help themselves overcome their attention problems.

Finally, in Chapter 9, the authors "put it all together" for the teen reader. The information in the book is blended and integrated into a plan for action.

Thank you, Ruth and Ken, for taking the effort to write this book. It will not only inform teens with ADHD, it will empower them with the necessary knowledge and sense of self that will help them truly *take control* of their ADHD.

—Larry B. Silver, M.D.,
Clinical Professor of Psychiatry,
Georgetown University Medical Center

INTRODUCTION

JAKE'S STORY

Jake was always getting in trouble. He didn't mean to act up; he just couldn't stop himself from moving and talking all of the time. It was like Jake had a motor inside of him that was always revving at high speed. In fact, his parents used to call him "Motor Man" because of the way he would run around the house with his toy cars and planes. And when he got an idea about something, Jake just could not stop himself from acting on it, such as the time when he was 6 years old and wanted to see how many LEGO bricks he could flush down the toilet. He wasn't *trying* to clog the toilet and flood the bathroom—but that's exactly what happened. His parents were really not happy with him that day.

When they weren't upset with him, his parents liked to tell stories of how they had to "Jake proof" the house when Jake was younger. For example, they put locks on all of the kitchen cabinets to keep 4-year-old Jake from getting into everything. They also talked about what a poor sleeper he was and how they used to end up with bruises from Jake kicking them in his sleep when he would climb into his parents' bed at night. Jake didn't like these stories because they made him feel like he was a loser. Even though his parents often told him that they loved him, he was still always getting in trouble. The two most frequent phrases he heard from his parents—and teachers—were "stop doing that" and "settle down." Jake was tired of being scolded all of the time.

Things weren't much better in school either. In fact, now that he's in ninth grade, things are worse than ever. Jake has a hard time paying attention and never seems to get his class work finished. Truth is, he's bored most of the time in class, especially when his teachers are presenting new information and Jake is supposed to be taking notes. He tries to listen, but before too long his mind starts drifting, and he ends up thinking about his upcoming baseball game or what he is going to do next weekend. When he isn't daydreaming in class, Jake is talking to his friends. It is bad enough that he gets in trouble for talking, but sometimes he gets his friends in trouble too. For example, his best friend, Mike, asked to have his seat changed in English class so that he could move away from Jake. In fact, many of Jake's friends are getting frustrated with him. He has lost count of the number of times his friends tell him to "chill" because he is talking too much or interrupting them when they are talking. Last week the whole baseball team got upset with him because he missed an easy fly ball when he was daydreaming instead of paying attention to the game.

ABBY'S STORY

Abby always forgot things. She forgot to bring her homework and books home with her after school. She forgot to do her homework because she got caught up watching TV or chatting with her friends on Facebook. Even when she did remember to do her homework, sometimes Abby forgot to turn it in. Her parents and teachers were constantly frustrated with her. They told her things like, "You need to apply yourself more" or "Your grades would be so much better if you tried harder." Although no one ever called her "lazy," Abby knew that's what was meant. Abby didn't understand why she was having so much trouble in school, but she knew one thing for certain: She *did not* like school. For instance, she hated getting up in the morning. When her alarm clock went off, Abby usually just hit the snooze button and went back to sleep until her mom came in and started yelling at her that she was going to be late. And Abby was always late. It took her a long time to get ready in the morning because she felt sluggish for at least an hour after waking up. Then there was the hunt for lost shoes, sweaters, books, and other items that she needed but couldn't remember where she had left them.

Abby hated sitting in class. She felt restless and antsy all of the time (maybe that's why all of her pencils were gnarled from her chewing on them). Instead of focusing on her teachers, Abby was always worrying about things. For instance, she didn't like Tuesdays because that was group project day, and Abby always had trouble getting along with the other group members.

If things at home and school weren't bad enough, Abby's social life hasn't been much better, especially since she started the eighth grade this year. Her friends tell her that she talks too much and acts rude. They also tell her that she doesn't seem to be interested in what they are talking about. But the biggest problem is that Abby can never keep a secret. Sooner or later, without meaning to, Abby usually blabs about something that she promised not to tell anyone. Abby doesn't realize it, but her friends are getting tired of her and don't want to spend time with her.

Abby and Jake are kids with ADHD. If you are reading this book, chances are you are a kid with ADHD too. You are in some pretty good company though. Many famous people have been diagnosed with ADHD or are believed to have had ADHD. They include Olympic swimming phenomenon Michael Phelps, singer Solange Knowles (sister of Beyoncé), singer and actor Justin Timberlake, celebrity chef Jamie Oliver, actors Will Smith and Jim Carrey, TV star Ty Pennington, and comedian and talk show host Howie Mandel.

This book is about you and for you. Just like these famous people have learned to cope with their attention problems and rise above them, this book will help you do the same. First, we will explain what ADHD is and how it develops in young people. We are mostly going to stay away from technical and scientific talk, but there are a few statistics that you need to know. For example, teenagers with ADHD are at a higher risk for having driving accidents, learning difficulties, and social problems. This doesn't mean that you are going to have any of these difficulties, but by understanding your ADHD better, you decrease the chances that you will have any of these complications. After we define ADHD and tell you what other problems you have to look out for, we will give you many strategies to help you deal with your ADHD. In fact, one of the best strategies is to create a lot of structure and external organization. So we are going to practice what we preach and give *you* some structure right now.

This book is divided into nine chapters that cover the following topic areas:

1. ADHD—What is it?
2. How did I get it?
3. What does it look like?
4. How long does it last?
5. What does treatment look like?
6. How do I get help at school?
7. How can technology help?
8. What can I do for myself?
9. Putting it all together

We are going to visit with Abby and Jake at the end of each chapter as they learn about ADHD and ways to deal with their attention problems. Other kids with ADHD who we have worked with over the years and are just like you will also share their thoughts and feelings. Their quotes will be scattered throughout the following chapters.

Before we start, here are a few things to consider when reading this book. First, we suggest reading the book along with a parent, counselor, or other trusted adult so you can share your reactions and feelings. It is often helpful to talk with someone about the information you have read because it becomes more meaningful and you can get his or her feedback and point of view on what you've read. Second, and most importantly, we want you to remember that you are a great person despite, because of, and regardless of your ADHD. ADHD does not define who or what you are. It is merely a part of you, like your sense of humor or athletic ability or any other characteristic you possess. Try to remember that as you read this book. Now let's get going!

CHAPTER 1

ADHD— WHAT IS IT?

"I prefer to distinguish ADD as attention abundance disorder. Everything is just so interesting . . . remarkably at the same time."

—Frank Coppola

Y ou may think that ADHD is a relatively new diagnosis and you have probably been told that more and more students are receiving this diagnosis. In fact, even though ADHD is one of the most common disorders seen in children, some people still question whether there really is such a thing. They say that if students simply worked harder, they would have no problems. Others are quick to say that the reason children aren't paying attention is because their teachers or parents are not doing their jobs. None of these assertions provides a valid explanation for ADHD. We now have evidence of biological differences in individuals with ADHD. It's not your parents' fault, your teachers' fault, or your fault anymore than it is your fault if your vision is weak and you have to wear glasses. To help you understand this better, we will discuss the definition of ADHD and how it is based on ways the brain works in Chapter 2.

More than 100 years ago, in 1902, Dr. George Still from Britain was the first one to describe a condition in which a child was inattentive, impulsive, and hyperactive (Barkley, 2006). Just like today, even then there were more boys than girls diagnosed with ADHD and symptoms seemed to occur before children were 7 years old. Dr. Still didn't believe that children were lazy or unmotivated; he believed that their internal biology was different. This was a revolutionary idea at the time and emphasized what we still believe today. Your biology (how your brain is organized) and your genetics (characteristics that your parents passed on to you) determine whether or not you have ADHD, not your intelligence or motivation.

Through years of research, we now know much more about ADHD since Dr. Still first did his work. We will discuss this information so you have a full understanding of what is involved. Even the terminology has changed—and is still changing for that matter.

The American Psychiatric Association's *Diagnostic and Statistical Manual of Mental Disorders* (*DSM*) is what most professionals use to diagnose many different kinds of conditions. Through the years, this manual has been revised and updated. We are now using the revised edition of the *DSM-IV*, and the *DSM-V* is currently in the works.

The terms and labels will sound strange to you but back in 1968, in the second edition of the *DSM*, what we now call ADHD was described as Hyperkinetic Reaction of Childhood Disorder, and experts believed that the "behavior usually diminishes by adolescence" (Barkley, 2006, p. 9). By 1986, however, it became clear that although the very active behavior or hyperactivity diminished by adolescence, often the difficulties with attention and impulsivity remained (Weiss & Hechtman, 1986). Because of the research, the name was changed to Attention Deficit Disorder With or Without Hyperactivity in the third edition of the *DSM* (which was published in 1980 by the American Psychiatric Association), indicating that you could have ADHD even without being hyperactive. In 1987, the definition was revised again to Attention Deficit/Hyperactivity Disorder; ADD Without Hyperactivity was considered a different diagnosis. Based on information in the next manual (the *DSM-IV*, published in 1994) and the subsequent revision (the *DSM-IV-TR*, published in 2000), we currently refer to three subtypes of ADHD: Predominantly Hyperactive-Impulsive Type, Predominantly Inattentive Type, and a Combined Type.

Despite the various attempts at definition and the research that accompanied the definitions, few changes were occurring in the schools; ADHD was considered primarily a medical condition. However, this all changed in 1990–1991 when the Individuals with Disabilities Education Act (IDEA) was revised so that students diagnosed with ADHD could receive special education services. Many of you may have an IEP or a 504 Plan that gives you accommodations in school. Your services and accommodations

The three types of ADHD are:
➤ ADHD, Predominantly Hyperactive-Impulsive Type;
➤ ADHD, Predominantly Inattentive Type; and
➤ ADHD, Combined Type.

For more information and examples of what ADHD is and what it looks like, check out the following website: http://faculty.washington.edu/chudler/adhd.html.

are based on aspects of these laws that were not available until the 1990s. We will be discussing these in more detail in Chapter 6.

HOW DO WE DIAGNOSE ADHD?

Your parents may have told you that you were a very active child who was "always into everything." Your teachers may have said that you "couldn't sit still" or "couldn't stay focused on your work." Even now, you may notice that you often daydream or lose concentration on what is in front of you, but does this mean you have ADHD? Lots of kids are active or have trouble with school-work. What makes you different from them?

Besides, there are things that you at-tend to very well. When something captures your interest, whether it's sports, a project, or a computer game, you pay attention as well as anyone else and sometimes even better than your friends. Everyone has trouble staying focused on something when they are bored or not interested. What makes you different from everyone else?

> "I can't sit still in my seat so I can't learn."
>
> —John, age 15

One of the reasons that the diagnosis of ADHD is not always clear is that there is not a blood test or an x-ray to support the diagnosis. When you have a fever and sore throat, your doctor can take a throat culture to see if you have strep throat. Because there is no ADHD germ or virus, psychologists and doctors, like the authors, can't use medical tests to diagnose it. We diagnose it from information gathered from your parents, your teachers, and you. People who know you very well fill out questionnaires about your behavior at home, in school, with your friends, when you go to a restaurant, or when you do your homework. We also get information about your medical history from when you were a small child up until now. We check to see if anyone in your fam-ily has had similar problems because we know that ADHD often runs in families. Sometimes, you may take a battery of tests that look at your learning and problem-solving styles, your academic skills, and your memory and organizational abilities. We may also ask you to play what seem to be games on the computer to see how quickly and accurately you respond. Then, your pediatrician, psychologist, or psychiatrist takes all of that information and compares it with the criteria listed in the DSM book we mentioned earlier.

The DSM lists certain characteristics that must be present before you can be diagnosed with ADHD. You must display a certain number of these characteristics. In addition, the symptoms have to be seen for at least 6 months and they have to have appeared before you were 7 years old. We find that about 3%–7% of all children in the U.S. actually meet the ADHD diagnostic criteria (American Psychiatric Association, 2000).

DIFFERENT KINDS OF ADHD

We're going to talk a little about the three types of ADHD in the DSM-IV-TR because it is important for you to know this information.

Here are the criteria for the Hyperactive-Impulsive Type:

➤ You often fidget with your hands or your feet may be bouncing up and down.
➤ You have a hard time staying in your seat, both at school and during dinnertime.
➤ When you were younger, you probably ran around a lot; now you work hard to stay still but you still feel very restless.
➤ You feel like you are "driven by a motor."
➤ You may talk a lot and find it is hard to stop.

Characteristics for the Inattentive Type are a little different. For example:

➤ You may have trouble paying attention to details or you may make careless mistakes at school or work.
➤ You often have trouble maintaining your attention to tasks in school or to other activities when you are playing.

➤ You have trouble listening when someone is talking to you, especially if he or she is saying something complicated.
➤ You have trouble following through with an assignment and finishing your work.
➤ You have problems with orga- nization and you are often losing things.
➤ You are easily distracted and often forget things you should have remembered.

"I daydream or talk to my friends about random things instead of focusing on the work."
—Sharon, age 12

If you have the Combined Type, then:
➤ You have characteristics of both the Hyperactive-Impulsive and Inattentive types.

WHAT MAKES YOU DIFFERENT?

Although many kids have some of these characteristics, there are critical differences between what they are experiencing and your experiences:
➤ You cannot simply will yourself to stay focused when you want to. As hard as you try and as motivated as you are, you cannot consistently stay focused and keep from being distracted.
➤ These difficulties interfere with your performance in a significant way in either one or several of these areas: socially with friends, academically in school, at home, or in other activities. They may affect how you interact with friends and whether you pick up on subtle social cues (e.g., like when someone looks away a lot while you are talking to him). They may interfere with your perfor- mance in school and with your ability to complete tests, write papers, or finish your homework. They may affect your performance on a job—you may be so late, disorga- nized, or distracted that you cannot do what is required.

➤ These traits or characteristics have to be present in more than one setting and since before you were 7 years old. For example, you can't have ADHD only in math class or only when you do your homework; it must be there in several different places on a regular basis.

WHAT IS THIS "ALPHABET SOUP"?

Attention Deficit Disorder or Attention Deficit/Hyperactivity Disorder (ADD/ADHD)

Predominantly Hyperactive-Impulsive Type (sometimes called ADHD-PHI)

Predominantly Inattentive Type (sometimes called ADHD-PI)

Combined Type (sometimes called ADHD-C)

All of these initials and terms can make things confusing, so let's take a closer look at what we are talking about.

THE HYPERACTIVE-IMPULSIVE PERSON—ADHD, PREDOMINANTLY HYPERACTIVE-IMPULSIVE TYPE

Individuals with this kind of ADHD are often identified at the youngest ages. Although young children are frequently very active, you must have been more active than the typical child to qualify as a child with ADHD-PHI. You may have been a child who never sat still when eating a meal, who was always on the go, or who had so much energy your parents or caretakers were exhausted and frustrated keeping track of you. You were likely a child who would run from one activity to another very quickly; at the playground you were on the monkey bars, the jungle gym, the seesaw, and then back to the monkey bars within minutes. Once you entered preschool, you had a hard time sitting still in "circle time" even though you often knew everything your teachers were talking about. If the teacher was reading a book to the class, you were likely walking or running around the room. Sometimes you would finish things very quickly—too quickly to do your best—but you couldn't slow down. Taking you to a restaurant was often a challenge because you needed to be up and walking around instead of waiting patiently for your food to be served. And when dinner did come, you were usually the first one done and couldn't wait quietly for everyone else to finish dinner. As you got older, your parents may have told you some of these stories with smiles on their faces, but when you were going through these events, they did not always feel so good. People were often yelling at you or asking you to do something that you just couldn't manage.

These issues can also affect your friendships. Other children are doing one thing at a time and you are racing around. You invade others' space by getting too close or in their face when you are talking to them. You are more like a bull in a china shop, wanting desperately to be included but not being able to adjust your activity level to be appropriate. You may have developed the reputation of being a bad kid because you couldn't pay attention and do what was being asked. As you got a little older the "H" (hyperactive) part of your personality started to be less obvious, but that didn't mean your mind was not racing. The difference was that your body was more able to stay in one place. You may have noticed that your leg was bouncing up and down as you were sitting or that you were tapping your pencil on the desk constantly, but at least you could stay in your seat (even if it took extra effort). Did that mean you no longer had ADHD? No, it simply meant that the outward signs changed as you got older. Even if your body was no longer always moving, it often still felt like you couldn't turn off your internal motor and you were constantly thinking of different ideas that distracted you from the task at hand.

THE INATTENTIVE PERSON—ADHD, PREDOMINANTLY INATTENTIVE TYPE

Children with this type of ADHD are often overlooked until they are a bit older. They are not physically overactive or do not demonstrate behavior problems so no one notices any issues. In fact, they often look like they are paying perfect attention, but their mind is wandering. If you were one of these children, you likely were told that you were "daydreaming," "spacy," "lazy," or just "not interested." Your parents or your teacher would give directions and you just didn't hear them. They would repeat directions again and again as they became more angry or frustrated with you until you finally registered what they were saying. You were not daydreaming or being "spacy" on purpose and you were not lazy or disinterested. In fact, you were probably very interested, but not in what was being presented just then. Your mind was distracted by something else. It might have been some passing noise in the hall, a bird flying by the window, or your thoughts about an afterschool activity. Your brain was having a hard time staying focused on a single point; it was as if multiple TV channels were playing in your head at the same time and you could not tune in to one at a time. Some of you may have seemed quiet, withdrawn, or anxious. Often more girls than boys are diagnosed with this form of ADHD.

When children are younger, teachers and parents often repeat information for everyone so your difficulties may not have been so noticeable, but this changed once you entered middle school. In middle school, directions are only given once or twice, and you are expected to finish your work in a limited amount of time. You probably aren't completing your work if you are easily distracted by other things and not focused on your assignment.

You may notice these problems occur in other places too, not just in school. Some children report that they have trouble focusing during a sports activity. This is especially true for games like soccer or baseball when you need to be paying attention to the play in case the ball comes your way. Many kids with this kind of attention issue find themselves thinking of something else and then are totally surprised and unprepared when they have to respond quickly.

You may be the best reporter for this kind of ADHD because so much of the distractibility is internal and you are the person most aware of it. It is important that you also don't fall into the trap of thinking you are simply "not a student" or "not smart." Your inattentive type of ADHD can prevent you from demonstrating the many strengths and talents that you have.

THE HYPERACTIVE AND INATTENTIVE PERSON—ADHD, COMBINED TYPE

Most teens with ADHD are diagnosed with the Combined Type. In fact, many younger children who are at first diagnosed with the Hyperactive-Impulsive Type are later diagnosed with the Combined Type as they get older and their symptoms and the expectations change.

If you fall in this category, you were likely an active child (as we described in the Hyperactive-Impulsive section), but as you got a bit older the hyperactivity diminished—yet you still had trouble staying focused and working slowly and carefully. You not only had difficulty following directions and listening like the students with the Inattentive Type, but you also rushed through your work making careless mistakes. This was often frustrating for your parents and teachers but also for you because you knew the material, but these impulsive mistakes lowered your grades. You knew that you were probably smarter than other students without these difficulties, but they were getting better grades. This often got you so frustrated that you were ready to give up, but if you did, you were the one who lost in the long run.

Now that you are older—in middle school and high school—organizational difficulties have become more obvious. You have to manage time and assignments from several teachers, you have to have the right books in the right classes, and you have to know how to plan for long-term projects so you don't procrastinate and stay up all night before a paper is due. Being able to develop a schedule becomes critical so you can juggle all of the academic and extracurricular activities you want to enjoy without your grades suffering. Some students are not identified until they hit this point because they have been able to compensate and get by on their smarts up until now. In fact, parents and teachers often don't identify these students as having ADHD—they think that they are so smart that they *can't* have ADHD. But ADHD is not a

In Chapter 9 you will be able to figure out what type of ADHD you have and how it specifically affects you.

function of intelligence; many gifted students have ADHD and cannot demonstrate their giftedness because of the symptoms.

WHERE IS JAKE?

Now that you know a little about how ADHD is diagnosed, you probably realize that when he was younger, Jake was identified with ADHD, Hyperactive-Impulsive Type. Now that he is in high school, that diagnosis has been changed to ADHD, Combined Type. This is because Jake isn't as active as he used to be and isn't always getting into trouble for not staying still; now he often can stay in his seat, but he is so distracted by things around him and by his own ideas that he cannot pay attention to what is going on. This can be very difficult both in class and with his friends, especially because Jake is a bright guy and everyone figures he could do it if he just wanted to. In fact, Jake was moved out of his Honors English class to a grade-level class because the teacher thought he was just being lazy and didn't care about completing his homework. Jake was distressed. He knew he was smart enough to do the work in the Honors class; he just couldn't manage his time to get the homework done each night.

WHERE IS ABBY?

Like many girls with ADHD (but not all), Abby is identified with ADHD, Predominantly Inattentive Type. The problem with this type of ADHD is that most of the time, people don't know that Abby is having more trouble than anyone else. She is not hyperactive like Jake; she sits quietly and does not cause anyone to notice her, but she often doesn't tune in to what is going on— either with friends or at home or school. She'll tell her friends she will meet them at a certain time and place, and then forgets all about it, so her friends get angry with her. Abby doesn't do this on purpose. One time, she planned to meet her friends, but as she was walking to their meeting place, she met someone else and stopped to talk, then she stopped to text another friend, and by the time she got to the meeting place, her friends had already left. Abby didn't want to miss her friends or to make them upset with her, but there were too many distractions along the way.

For Jake and Abby and for you, the first step to helping yourself is knowing what the problem is. If you have read this chapter, you probably recognized some familiar patterns, some comments that you have heard, and some behaviors with which you have trouble. Maybe a parent or your doctor has already told you that you are a person with ADHD and what type of ADHD you have. Now that you know more about the diagnosis, you can understand the kinds of things that may be harder for you because of it. In later chapters, we will be giving you some strategies and methods to help you overcome these problems so they don't cause you as much difficulty as they do now.

Highlights and Recap

➤ Individuals with the behaviors we are now calling ADHD were first identified in 1902, although it was first defined formally in 1968.

➤ There is scientific evidence that ADHD is a biologically based disorder—it does not come from poor teaching or parenting. It does not reflect a lack of intelligence, motivation, or effort on the part of the student.

➤ Terminology and classifications of ADHD have changed over the years. Currently, three subtypes are defined: Predominantly Hyperactive-Impulsive Type, Predominantly Inattentive Type, and Combined Type. Often there are more boys than girls labeled with the Hyperactive-Impulsive Type and more girls than boys identified with the Inattentive Type; these labels may change as students get older.

➤ It was not until 1990–1991 that formal services for ADHD in schools became available.

➤ Three to seven percent of children in the U.S. are identified with ADHD. It is the most commonly diagnosed disorder among children.

CHAPTER 2

HOW DID I GET IT?

"Ah, the clock is always slow,
it is later than you think."
—Robert W. Service

f you are like most kids with ADHD, you have probably asked yourself, "Why me? What did I do wrong to get this disorder?" Let's be clear about something: You didn't do anything wrong. ADHD is not the result of laziness, poor study habits, lack of motivation, or faulty character. You didn't "catch" ADHD from someone at school either. ADHD is not a virus or a germ that can be spread. And you didn't get ADHD from something you ate. Although you may have seen ads on TV or in magazines that claim ADHD is caused by eating too much sugar or having too much red dye in your diet (you don't think that Twizzlers are that color naturally, do you?), there is no evidence that sugar or food additives cause ADHD. Other people say that ADHD comes from watching too much TV or playing too many video games. Not true. Finally, some people claim that the way you are raised leads to ADHD. Although the way you are raised does play a role in your behavior, it does not cause ADHD.

Although all of these theories are bogus, they contain some true facts. For example, some people get a sugar buzz when they eat too much candy and become hyperactive. Similarly, an allergy to a specific food or food additive can make someone hyperactive. However, there is no proof that environmental or social factors (i.e., where you were raised or how you were raised) cause ADHD.

So what does cause ADHD? The truth is that no one really knows how ADHD develops or why you have it when your brother or sister does not. We do know that boys are more likely to be diagnosed than girls and that the number of people with ADHD is equal across races, cultures, and countries. ADHD is not just an American problem. In every developed nation in the world, about 5% of children are diagnosed with ADHD (Barkley, 2008).

So if environmental, parenting, and cultural differences don't cause ADHD, then what does? Most scientists believe that heredity (your genes) and biology (how your brain develops) cause ADHD. This means that the way the brain develops has a lot to do with who has ADHD and who does not. In fact, Dr. Russell Barkley (2008) said that ADHD is one of the "top 3 genetically predisposed disorders in all of psychiatry." Dr. Barkley and many other researchers believe that there are multiple biologically based causes, or in other words, many different combinations of factors that lead to ADHD. Think about it this way: Imagine that your brain is a large park with many different, intersecting paths. Now imagine that ADHD is a basketball court somewhere in that park. ADHD researchers believe that just like there are many different paths that lead to the basketball court, there are many different paths that lead to ADHD. That's why no two individuals with ADHD ever have exactly the same symptoms. It's called heterogeneity [het'ər ō' jə nē'ə tē] and one way to think about it is to consider snowflakes. Although no two snowflakes look exactly alike (they are heterogeneous), they are all still snowflakes. Heterogeneity is why one child with ADHD has problems with impulsivity, but can pay attention pretty well, while another child can't pay attention at all, but doesn't have a problem with acting before thinking.

THE BRAIN AND ADHD

Although we do not know exactly what causes ADHD, most professionals agree that there are two types for ADHD to develop: acquired and inherited. In acquired ADHD, the developing baby's brain has been influenced in some way while still in the mother's womb or very soon after birth. That's why the term *acquired* is used; these babies were developing normally until something happened to alter the normal course of development. For example, we know from research that babies who are born prematurely, are small for their gestational age, and experience bleeding in the brain are at significantly higher risk for acquiring ADHD (Nigg, 2006). Similarly, children who have been treated for cancer with chemotherapy are at a higher risk for acquiring ADHD. Another way that children acquire ADHD is when their brains are exposed to some kind of toxin while still in their mother's womb. For example, we worked with a 15-year-old adopted girl at our office whose biological mother smoked cigarettes and drank alcohol throughout her pregnancy. Both cigarettes and alcohol have been linked to many developmental problems in infants, including ADHD. In the case of this girl, these toxins likely affected her early brain development and the combination of the two greatly increased her risk for acquiring ADHD. Finally, children who have had some type of traumatic brain injury like the kind resulting from a car accident or a serious concussion can have ADHD symptoms.

Although some children acquire their ADHD, the numbers are few compared to the second type. The majority of ADHD cases, about two-thirds to three-fourths, are caused by heredity.

> "My mom says my dad and I are just alike—neither one of us can sit through dinner without getting up at least three or four times."
>
> —Juan, age 14

This theory states that the brain develops differently because of the genes children inherit from their parents. Although a scientific review of the brain and genetics is beyond the scope of this book, let's review some information on the brain and what heredity means.

The brain is the most complex machine ever created. Our brains contain billions of cells, called neurons. Each neuron sends messages to other neurons, making billions upon billions of different connections or pathways. These neuron pathways control everything from telling your lungs to breathe, to helping you remember that 5 x 6 = 30, to reminding you that you really love your little brother so you don't get angry with him for playing with your laptop. How your brain develops and what neuron pathways are created are determined by your genes. A gene is like a bit of code or information. You inherit your genes from your parents; one set from each parent. These genes interact to determine everything about you from your eye and hair color, to how tall you are, to how susceptible you are to getting sunburned. For example, have you ever noticed that you have some of the same talents and skills that one or both of your parents have? That's the influence of genes and heredity. These same genes also influence the number and type of connections that the brain's neurons make. Certain genetic configurations are thought to lead to a pattern of behaviors that we know as ADHD.

Although we are learning more and more information about genes every day, no one yet knows which genes are responsible for ADHD. However, it is believed that multiple genes are involved and that ADHD is determined by the number and combination of these genes that are present. The more of these genes that are present, the greater the likelihood you will develop ADHD. Also, the particular combination of involved genes may influence which type of ADHD you have. This variability may explain why no two people with ADHD will have exactly the same pattern of symptoms. To make things even more complicated, just having the right number and combination of genetic markers does not necessarily mean someone will develop ADHD. It just means that the chances are greater. Remember, we don't know exactly what causes ADHD—this is just a theory.

Now that we know the two types of ADHD development, let's talk about where and how these genes are impacting brain development. The human brain is a very complex organ that has many parts. These parts are connected to each other through the neuron pathways that we talked about earlier.

Up until recently, it has been difficult to examine how the brain works because doctors could not get access to it. Unlike a blood test, which can tell us how much or how little of something we have in our blood, the brain does not reveal its secrets so easily. In the past, the only way to study it was to cut someone's brain open and start poking around. However, with the development of advanced imaging techniques (e.g., CT scans, MRI, fMRI), the brain could be examined without opening someone's head. As a result, there have been many studies (and many more going on right now and planned for the future) that compare the shape, size, and activity levels of different brains. For ADHD studies, researchers gather together a bunch of kids with ADHD and scan their brains. Then they compare those scans with the brain scans of a group of kids who do not have ADHD. Once they control for other factors, any differences between the two sets of scans can be concluded to result from ADHD. In other words, they can see how the different genes impact how the brain develops.

There are four major areas of the brain that are thought to be involved in ADHD: the prefrontal cortex, the basal ganglia, the limbic system, and the reticular activating system. Figure 1 shows a diagram of the brain with the relative location of these four sections.

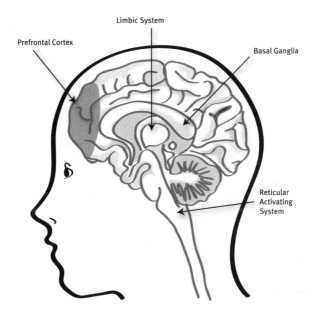

Figure 1. ADHD in the brain.

THE PREFRONTAL CORTEX (PFC)

The prefrontal cortex or PFC is located at the front of your brain, behind your eyes and forehead. It is a very important structure that has connections to many other brain structures. Because of these extensive connections, the PFC is kind of like the brain's coach. Just like a softball team needs a good coach to coordinate the play of all of its team members, the PFC helps to coordinate many of your behaviors. This coordinating ability is called executive functioning (covered in the next chapter), and executive functioning is closely related to ADHD. Basically, the PFC is involved in working memory, planning, impulse control, and emotion regulation, all executive functions.

For example, let's look at what you need to do to write a paper for school. To write an effective thesis, you have to keep the topic and main point in mind from beginning to end (working memory). You need to plan and organize your paper so it flows logically (planning), resist the impulse to go outside and play basketball with your friends (impulse control), and control your irritation with your teacher for giving you this lousy homework assignment in the first place (emotional regulation). Without good executive functioning skills, you cannot do all of these tasks simultaneously. People with ADHD often have difficulty with these executive functions. The PFC of people with ADHD is underactive—there is less activity going on in this part of the brain than in the brains of people who don't have ADHD. One reason for this underactivity is that the PFC of kids with ADHD develops more slowly than the PFC of kids without it and may never catch up.

THE BASAL GANGLIA

This funnily named structure is located in the center of the brain, behind and below the prefrontal cortex (the cortex is the wrinkly section that looks like pizza with the cheese scraped off). The basal ganglia is one of the inhibition and control centers of the brain. It is connected to the PFC by many neuron paths. The basal ganglia receives signals from other parts of the brain that are associated with motor control, motivation, and emotion. These signals are then sent up to the PFC for further analysis. The PFC then sends signals down to the basal ganglia, in a sense telling the basal ganglia how to act upon the information. Studies have shown that the path or loop between the basal ganglia and the PFC does not function the same way in individuals with ADHD as it does in those without it. For example, let's say you are sitting at the dinner table and your basal ganglia is getting a lot of messages to move around or fidget. Normally, when the PFC receives those messages, it will tell the basal ganglia to ignore or suppress the messages so you can stay still through dinner. But because the feedback loop doesn't operate correctly in individuals with ADHD, those fidget messages don't get suppressed and you can't sit still.

THE LIMBIC SYSTEM

The limbic system refers to a group of structures located in the very center of the brain, under the basal ganglia. Perry (1998) called the limbic system the "emotional processing unit" of the brain because one of its jobs is to evaluate how to respond to emotional stimulation. Like the basal ganglia, the limbic system is heavily connected to the PFC and the feedback loop that it creates with the PFC helps you to remain focused. A very simplified explanation is that the limbic-PFC loop helps you to ignore information (e.g., I'm hungry, I hope that spider doesn't come over here) so you can remain focused on something else, like studying for your history test. As in the basal ganglia, the limbic system of individuals with ADHD is often underactive. Because of this, people with ADHD have a hard time ignoring emotional signals when they are trying to focus on activities.

THE RETICULAR ACTIVATING SYSTEM (RAS)

The reticular activating system or RAS is part of the brain stem, a stalk-like structure that extends down into the neck. The brain stem is considered part of the "old brain" structures that formed early in evolutionary development. The brain stem is involved in controlling movements, regulating consciousness, and processing nerve signals from all over the body. The RAS is called the attention center because of its role in regulating arousal or alertness. Again, the RAS is heavily connected to the PFC and the two help us to maintain our attention when needed.

You may have noticed a pattern in the descriptions of these brain structures—the PFC is closely associated with the other three. That's why the PFC is called the brain's coach and plays such a central role in executive functioning and ADHD. Philip Shaw and his colleagues (2007) at the National Institute of Mental Health compared brain scans of children (ages 6 to 16) with ADHD with scans of children who did not have ADHD. They found that in the ADHD brains, the PFC developed an average of 3 years later than in the non-ADHD brains. This study provided evidence of where and how ADHD affects brain development.

WHERE IS JAKE?

There are no other people in Jake's family with ADHD. His mother and father never had difficulties in school and none of Jake's aunts, uncles, or cousins have any attention issues. However, while pregnant with Jake, his mother got a very bad strep infection.

Also, he was born 2 months prematurely and spent 6 weeks in a neonatal intensive care unit because he was so small (he was even small for a premature baby). All of these factors likely influenced Jake's development of ADHD.

WHERE IS ABBY?

Abby's early development was fine. Her mother had no problems during the pregnancy, and Abby was born on time with no complications. Abby's ADHD was not acquired. In fact, Abby comes from a long line of children with ADHD. Abby is very much like her father was when he was a young boy. Abby's grandmother says that Abby's father also had trouble sitting still, doing his classwork, and getting along with other children when he was a child. And Abby and her father are not the only ones with ADHD in the family. Abby's older brother was diagnosed with ADHD when he was 6 years old, and she has two older cousins who take medication for ADHD.

Highlights and Recap

➤ ADHD is not caused by anything you ate, did, or didn't do. In some cases, ADHD can be acquired if a fetus or infant is exposed to some toxin that damages brain development. It can also be acquired as a result of brain injury.

➤ Most cases of ADHD are the result of a combination of heredity (genes) and biology (how the brain develops).

➤ The exact genes that cause ADHD have not yet been identified.

➤ ADHD is associated with four major areas or structures of the brain: the prefrontal cortex, the basal ganglia, the limbic system, and the reticular activating system.

➤ The prefrontal cortex plays a central role in ADHD.

➤ According to recent research, the prefrontal cortex is less active in people diagnosed with ADHD.

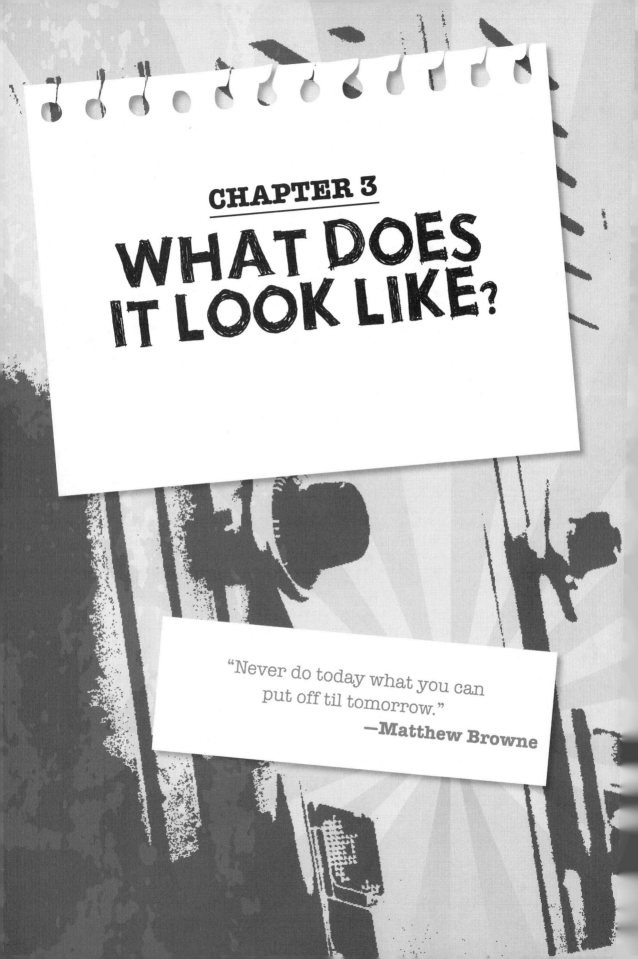

CHAPTER 3

WHAT DOES IT LOOK LIKE?

"Never do today what you can put off til tomorrow."

—Matthew Browne

Because ADHD is genetically based, it is part of who you are and it is with you in many different places: at home, at school, with your friends, when you are playing sports, or when you are at a party. But in each of these cases, different issues may arise. Remember the different types of ADHD: Hyperactive-Impulsive Type, Inattentive Type, and Combined Type? Each type has challenges associated with it, which may cause you different problems. In addition, just because two people have ADHD does not mean that their issues are the same.

Let's look at how Jake's and Abby's ADHD affects what happens with them in various situations. Jake is sometimes impulsive and talks too much in class. This gets him in trouble but also gets his friend in trouble when his friend isn't doing anything wrong, which was why his friend asked to have his seat moved. Abby has real trouble managing her time. She often gets to school late. Her parents get angry with her but she also misses important information in her classes. Abby does not remember deadlines for assignments and even misses appointments she makes with her friends. Naturally, her friends get upset with her and after a while, they don't want to include her in their plans because they always have to wait for her to show up.

Now let's look at how the symptoms may impact you so you can learn how to prevent them from interfering with your success and happiness. When you were younger, you probably had problems sitting still or you were always interrupting people. Although you may have outgrown these behaviors or learned ways of coping with these problems, you may now be dealing with other challenges. Here are some examples.

MANAGING TIME

Because you have a lot of energy, you also likely have lots of interests and enjoy many activities. But that means you have to manage your time wisely to get everything done and that can be difficult. Students with ADHD often have serious difficulty managing their time. You may need time for completing homework, playing sports, talking to friends, and participating in some other activities like drama or music. All that and you have to be in school 6 or 7 hours a day. No wonder you feel like there is not time to get everything done! You may have learned to make a schedule and do some of the other things we will discuss more fully in Chapters 5 and 6, but you often find it difficult to judge how long something will take—making your schedule less useful even if you have one. Your parents get angry and frustrated because you are taking so long to complete what is supposed to be a short assignment; they don't seem to realize that you are trying but your distractibility gets in the way. You may have a hard time staying focused to complete the work. For example, when working on the computer, you are often tempted to IM your friends or update your Facebook status. You may decide to make a new iPod playlist to study by, or you may just decide to lie down on your bed for a while. All of these distractions keep you from getting your work done. Have you ever noticed that you do better when you have a short deadline? Many ADHD students need the pressure of time to work effectively. If you have a long time to complete an assignment, you may tend to procrastinate until the last minute and you seem only to manage when the pressure is on right before the assignment is due. A deadline imposes a structure and immediacy to the assignment, which makes it easier for you to stay focused. It may not be the best way to work but it is often how you get things done.

Managing time in school is critical. First, you have to get there on time in the morning. In some schools, you are only allowed a certain number of days of being tardy before you get a detention or some other penalty. Similar problems come up when you are going from class to class. If you have to go to a locker to change books for the next class, you may take longer to remember and organize the books you need to take with you, or you may get distracted by talking to friends and arrive late to class. Again, some teachers lower your grades when you are late. Even if your grade is not affected, it means you are not there to get organized at the beginning of the class and to hear the instructions. This may be a bigger problem for you because, as we will discuss later, being organized itself is probably a challenge for you.

You may also find that you are not completing assignments that were meant to be finished in class. Then you have to take them home to finish, and that lengthens your homework time. This problem can become even more serious if you are not completing tests on time. Although you know all of the information, your grade won't reflect your knowledge if you don't complete the test because you are getting distracted. You may even see students who are not as smart or well prepared as you are that get a better grade, which becomes very frustrating.

Difficulties managing time can also interfere with your social relationships. If your friends are planning to meet at 4 p.m. and, like Abby, you are not there on time, they will likely start without you. If you are late to meet a carpool to go to a game or practice, your ride may have left by the time you get there. This can lead to your friends or teammates feeling that you don't care about them or are irresponsible and cannot be counted on. In fact, you are responsible and can be counted on, but you get distracted and lose track of time.

RESTLESSNESS

Although you are no longer hyperactive and don't move around all of the time like you did when you were younger, your mind may be restless and you may find yourself thinking of other things when you should be listening or focusing on an activity.

Do you notice that parents or siblings tell you things again and again before you hear them? There is nothing wrong with your hearing; you are simply focused on something else. Often you listen to the beginning of what they say and something in their comment makes you think of another idea, so it becomes even harder to stay focused. For example, if your mom is telling you about plans for dinner and you immediately associate it with what

"When I was a kid, I couldn't sit still. Now I can get through a whole class without getting out of my seat, but I still have trouble paying attention to the teacher."

—Julie, age 11

you had for lunch, the friend you were sitting with at lunch, and the conversations you had, and then realize you were supposed to call that friend, you have totally tuned out what your mom was telling you. Although other people can often "shelve" a thought and come back to it later (what we call using "working memory"), you have more trouble doing that. What is in your head at that moment is what governs your attention.

At school, a similar pattern can cause even more difficulty. If you don't hear what the teacher is saying because of your restless mind, you won't know what work to do and may miss the fact that there will be a test on Friday.

ATTENTION TO DETAILS

Paying attention to details may not sound very important but let's look at how often it affects you. If you misread or skip a word or line when reading, you won't understand what you have read accurately. This can also affect math if you add instead of subtract or misread the information in directions or word problems. If you omit a plus or minus sign on a number, or a parenthesis in an equation, you will get the answer wrong. This can affect your schoolwork, but it can also affect your everyday life. You may misunderstand a note from a parent, teacher, or friend. You may misunderstand directions for a recipe or for how to download a song. Parents or teachers will call you careless, even if you were trying as hard as you could.

Paying attention to details matters most when you start driving. You must pay attention to traffic lights, stop signs, speed limits, other cars on the road, and landmarks all at the same time. Barkley (1993) and Barkley and Murphy (1996, 2002) compared driving records of individuals with ADHD with records for drivers with similar experience without ADHD. Significantly more of the drivers with ADHD had received tickets, had been cited for speeding, and had their licenses suspended or revoked. Being able to stay focused on details when you are driving is a matter of safety for you and others. This does not mean you cannot be a good driver but it means you need to develop particular strategies to avoid these problems.

IMPULSIVITY

Impulsivity refers to your rushing into things without thinking or planning. Younger, impulsive children may seem fearless or reckless when in fact they just don't realize the consequences of their actions. They tackle equipment in the playground way beyond their skill level or they start a fight with a bigger child. They do not look for cars before crossing the street. Notably, not everybody with ADHD is impulsive.

Unless kids who are impulsive are treated, these problems may remain difficulties even when they are older. In preschool, impulsivity interferes mostly during playtime, which doesn't count so much. Now that you are older, it may cause you to blurt out answers before the question has been completed. This may result in two problems: First, you may get the wrong answer because you did not wait to get all of the information and second, others may get angry at you for answering out of turn and not giving them a chance to talk.

Similar difficulties may arise in other arenas. You may start playing the music prematurely if you are in a band or orchestra; you may take a shot in basketball when it is clear you can't make it; you may not complete both steps in a two-part math problem. Again, driving may pose a special problem. For example, if you resume driving before the light has changed, or if you don't give the right of way to pedestrians or other drivers, you could cause an accident.

EXECUTIVE FUNCTIONING

Executive functioning often goes along with ADHD. Executive functioning is an umbrella term used to describe higher level cognitive abilities that mediate a person's overall ability to utilize and demonstrate intellectual capabilities. Included in this domain are

behavioral controls (impulsivity, emotions, regulating work efforts) and cognitive controls (monitoring and modifying attention and effort level, planning ahead, managing time, following
through on tasks, or-
ganizing materials).

Several years ago,
Martha   Denckla
(1996) gave the anal-
ogy of a disheveled
cook as someone
with difficulties in
executive function-
ing. Imagine a cook
who has a well-sup-
plied kitchen with
all of the need-

Executive functioning: Just like an orchestra needs a good conductor to make sure that everyone in the orchestra plays together and makes beautiful music and not noise, we need well-developed executive functioning skills to decide how to plan, organize, and execute complex tasks.

ed ingredients on the shelves and a cookbook with the recipe.
However, this person does not get out all of the necessary ingredients ahead of time. The meat is not defrosted and the oven has
not been turned on to preheat. If this is what's happening, there
is no way the meal will be prepared on time even though all of
the ingredients are there and the person is clearly bright and really wants to make this recipe. It's a picture of someone who just
cannot get it together. We would say this person has difficulties
in executive functioning.

Although professionals don't all agree about the specific
problems that are included in what we call executive functioning, most theories share many of the same characteristics. Russell
Barkley (2006) looked at executive functions as a "specific class
of self-directed actions by the individual that are being used for
self-regulation toward the future" (pp. 304–305). He wrote that
executive functioning is deficient in all individuals with ADHD
because the ADHD disrupts the development and effective performance of the executive functions. He went on to say there
are four types of executive functions. Although he listed many
aspects of executive functioning, here are some that are specifically relevant for our discussion.

Regardless of whose definition we use, many items included in this category are similar for most researchers. The ones we will refer to include:

➤ *activation*: getting started on your work;

➤ *working memory*: holding information in your mind while manipulating it or while you are doing something else, like solving a math problem mentally;

➤ *organization*: organizing time or information or materials;

➤ *response inhibition*: being able to withhold a prepared response when it is not relevant to the situation or the problem (This goes along with the impulsivity we discussed earlier in this chapter. If you are impulsive, you have a very hard time exercising response inhibition.);

➤ *making transitions*: changing activities or your focus from one thing to another; and

➤ *emotional modulation*: exercising control over your emotions; either overreacting or not reacting at all.

Executive functioning clearly plays a role in many parts of your life. For example, activation is necessary to get you started on tasks. Once you get started, you must also maintain your focus and attention to be effective. Working memory and organization are both important in order to have good comprehension when you are reading. You must first use your working memory to remember the events that occurred and the information that you have already read. You must then organize the information so you can see the big picture (get the main idea). Although you could take notes when you read to help your working memory, students often just try to keep everything in their minds. That means they must not be distracted or they will forget about what they were thinking.

In written work, you must again organize information and be able to sequence events appropriately. Everyone has learned that to write an effective paragraph, you need a topic sentence at the beginning, a few supporting details, and a summary sentence. This is a method to help you organize your thoughts as you write. Response inhibition is called for to make sure you stay on topic and don't go off on tangents. In the same way that you make transitions in your own life, you need to provide transitions between paragraphs or sections when you are writing and develop the topic so the reader can follow your discussion. These are all aspects of executive functioning.

Math also has its own requirements for executive functioning. Solving just about all math problems requires an understanding of the sequence of steps; this becomes more complex as math skills become more sophisticated. If you solve an algebraic equation without attending to the correct sequence, your answer will be incorrect. Solving word problems also requires several aspects of executive functioning. First, you must be able to analyze the problem to know what you do first, second, and third. Then you have to organize the information into one or more equations to derive an answer and then you must again sequence the steps accurately to get the right answer.

Study skills, which are vital in middle school, high school, and beyond, also require many executive functioning skills. In order to complete homework successfully, you must hear the assignment accurately and get it written down in a timely manner (using your working memory). Then you must bring home the right books and remember what the tasks are. Once you are home, you must be able to activate (get started) and stay focused until you finish; each of these steps is difficult for students with ADHD and executive functioning weaknesses. In addition to daily homework and assignment completion, perhaps the tasks that require the most executive functioning are writing a research paper and studying for final exams. You may have noticed that you can tackle short papers and quizzes successfully but larger, more comprehensive tasks become overwhelming. That is because they require even more working memory and organization for you to be successful.

In addition, because working memory refers to the ability to hold information in your mind, it is critical for successful note taking from lectures. You need to hold what the speaker said in your mind and write it down while at the same time listening to the next comment the speaker is making. This can be very difficult for students with ADHD and executive functioning problems and has led to a frequent accommodation that gives these students a duplicate set of classroom notes (see Chapter 6).

We bet at least some of these problems seem familiar to you and so we will be discussing strategies to address them in Chapters 6 and 7—be sure to read those chapters carefully. We will show you ways to address these problems so they don't have to stand in your way.

WHERE IS JAKE?

Jake's ADHD and executive functioning difficulties have caused serious problems in school for him. Time management is a particularly difficult area for Jake—he never completes his classwork and that means he often has extra work to do at home. In addition, he has difficulty completing tests so that even though he is smart, his grades don't show it. Teachers often are not sympathetic, feeling that because he is so smart, he could do his work if he would just stop talking to his friends and stay focused, but he can't.

Jake's history teacher also grades students on the quality of their notes. Because Jake is so easily distracted, his notes are usually incomplete. He may get the first few sentences of the discussion, but then he starts thinking about something else and loses focus on what the teacher is saying. Even when he is focused, he has working memory problems so it is particularly hard for him to hold on to what the teacher is saying long enough to write it down accurately, and if he does, he misses the next couple of sentences. He might understand it better and remember more if he could just listen and not have to write anything down, but the teacher is grading him on his notes so he has to take them.

WHERE IS ABBY?

Several of Abby's difficulties can be traced to problems typically associated with ADHD, Inattentive Type, and executive functioning issues. Her time management is very problematic so she does not get to school on time and she has not been taught strategies to allow her to change that behavior. Once she gets to school, her organizational difficulties become apparent and she loses papers, forgets to bring the right books to class, and doesn't remember to hand in her homework even when she finished it the night before.

Abby also gets distracted when she is talking with her friends so they get upset with her. It is very hard for her to inhibit her responses so she will share private information that she was asked to keep secret. It's not that Abby doesn't understand what her friends want; she knows the importance of secrets and privacy. It's just that before she knows it, she has blurted out something she didn't mean to say. Her friends get very angry with her; they're sure she is just doing it to make them angry and don't understand that she cannot help herself. If this continues, Abby will lose her friends.

Highlights and Recap

➤ Although the outward symptoms of ADHD may change as you get older, aspects of it remain with you throughout your life.

➤ These symptoms can affect you throughout your day at home, at school, and with your friends.

➤ Five major symptoms of ADHD are managing your time, restlessness, attention to details, impulsivity, and executive functioning problems.

➤ You may already have learned some ways of coping with these problems. In Chapters 6 and 7 we will give you even more strategies and talk about how technology can help so these difficulties don't have to interfere with who you are or what you want to achieve for yourself.

CHAPTER 4

HOW LONG DOES IT LAST?

"I'm sorry . . . I wasn't paying attention
to what I was thinking."

—Shelley Curtiss

Now that you know what ADHD is, how it developed, and how it affects you, one thing you may be wondering is whether you can get rid of it. We are going to be honest with you—chances are that your ADHD will follow you into adulthood. A very large research study followed kids with ADHD as they grew up (Barkley, Murphy, & Fischer, 2008). This study found that about 66% of these kids still struggled with their ADHD symptoms into adulthood. Although that means that 34% did not, it makes more sense to assume that you are going to be in the first group.

So how does ADHD change as you get older? For many of you with ADHD, you may have noticed that you have an easier time sitting still, but organization problems remain and get bigger. This is partly because as you grow older, school and parent expectations increase. However, it is also because your internal distractibility does not decrease along with the decrease in restlessness. But because you *look* like you are paying attention, parents and teachers expect that you *are* paying attention and don't offer as much support and guidance anymore. That's why you need to learn specific skills and strategies that will help you be more independent and effective.

While you are still in middle school or even high school, your parents are probably making sure that you take your medication, eat right, and meet regularly with your tutor. But once you graduate from high school, there will be no one following up with you to make sure that you continue to do these things. That responsibility will fall on your shoulders alone. That's why it's very important that you learn as much about ADHD as you can now so you will know how to take control of these issues when you are older.

There is a lot of research about kids with ADHD. There is also a lot of recent information about people who are not diagnosed with ADHD until they are older. However, there is not much data that focuses on what challenges await students with ADHD after they graduate high school and how they can meet these challenges.

To be successful, most of you reading this book will still need to be doing all of the strategies we will be talking about in Chapters 6 and 7 when you are attending college, embarking on your career, getting married, and having kids. But there is some good news: If you continue to take medication (if it is helpful), work with a coach, keep yourself organized, and stay alert, studies have shown that your ADHD will have little negative effect on your life. Think of it this way: If an athlete trains, watches his weight, and works out regularly, he is in peak condition. But if he stops training and doesn't work out for a period of time, he regresses and very quickly gets out of shape. He can start his training again and regain his strength but he must continue doing this on a regular basis to maintain his condition. The same thing is true with ADHD. If you don't continue using the strategies you know work for you, you will regress and have difficulties.

Here are a few problems that can develop in adulthood for those who stop taking care of their ADHD when they grow up. Some of these were discussed in Chapter 3 when we talked about what ADHD looks like for you now as a student. Without continued training and use of the strategies you have learned, these same difficulties will interfere into college and adulthood.

EXECUTIVE FUNCTIONING

You had to demonstrate executive functioning even when you were younger when you tuned in to one thing at a time, finished your homework on time, planned an activity, or cleaned up your room. As you began middle school and high school, expectations increased, and now you have to plan long-term projects, organize information to study for final exams, or complete a research paper. You often have to juggle a very busy schedule with activities, homework, and responsibilities at home without forgetting something or being late. Problems with executive functioning often go hand in hand with ADHD and so you may have worked with a coach to help you improve these skills. Coaches continue working with individuals throughout different life stages. In addition to the coaches for sports teams that you know about, there are also life coaches, job coaches, and people like therapists or counselors who guide individuals in their marriages or in learning parenting skills. Many people who do not have ADHD also find this kind of coaching or counseling helpful, but for adults with ADHD, it often means the difference between success and failure. As we discussed in Chapter 3, there are many different aspects of executive functioning. Without good strategies to overcome your weaknesses in executive functioning, they will continue to impact you as you get older. Let's discuss some of these potential problem areas.

GETTING STARTED

One aspect of executive functioning that you may have trouble with is getting started on tasks; we call it activation. You can think about it in physics terms. Inertia is the term used to explain that a body at rest tends to stay at rest until a force acts upon it that is strong enough to make it move. Sometimes it can take a small force to make you move, but other times it is very difficult to overcome inertia. You want to accomplish a task but just can't get yourself to begin. It may look like you are unmotivated, but in fact, you just can't focus enough or organize the information effectively to know how to begin. Often medication can help with this problem or if you have worked with a coach, you may have learned some strategies to begin tasks. Adults with ADHD often still have this problem so they need to continue using their strategies and/or take medication or this lack of activation can become a serious problem at home, at school, and at work. If you can't start a task, clearly you never finish it and get the grade or salary you deserve.

PRIORITIZING

As you get older, you become more independent and there are even more things on your "to do" list. When you were younger, someone else did your laundry, cooked your meals, and reminded you to take your medication. Now you have to do many of these things yourself. But we know that organizing and prioritizing are difficult tasks for individuals with ADHD. Whether you have learned to develop calendars, color code items by their level of importance, or learned a different system, you have probably figured out some way to know what is most important to do first. You will need to continue using these systems in college as you get multiple assignments all due at the same time, or at work, when you have several projects to be accomplished by a deadline. To get them done on time so you don't lose credit in college, or you don't get a poor evaluation at work, you will need a system that works for you. You may be saying, "Wait, but I'm not in college yet." We'd like to emphasize to you that these issues don't disappear just because you are an adult—so now is the time to learn effective strategies to cope!

TIME MANAGEMENT

Once you have developed priorities, you need to be able to estimate how long something will take so your schedule is realistic. You need to factor in all of the time commitments you have so that you do this accurately. If you are working on a project for geography class, then you need to build in time for both report preparation and delivery of the project. Simply doing the work will not earn any credit if the report is not completed and delivered on time. You also have to take into account that you may be more easily distracted than others and so specific projects may take you longer. That extra time also needs to be built into your schedule. Many people with ADHD have serious difficulty keeping track of time and adhering to a schedule. Whether you have alarms on your watch or cell phone, or have developed another system, you need to be aware that most people with ADHD simply cannot rely on their good intentions alone to get something done. You need strategies to help overcome these particular difficulties.

MANAGING YOUR FINANCES

Managing money requires conscientious tracking and attention to detail—both of which are difficult for many people with ADHD. Again, when you were younger, your parents may have given you an allowance so you didn't have this major responsibility. However, now that you are older you may be looking at getting a part-time job in the summer, you may earn some extra money doing odd jobs for your neighbor, or your allowance and savings may have grown bigger than your hiding place in your bedroom, making you want to get a bank account.

In some ways, technology has simplified this process but in other ways, it has complicated it. In the past, most people had a single checkbook or credit card, and most purchases were made in the store with cash, meaning that there were only a few things to coordinate. Now many people pay bills and complete other bank transactions online, take cash from the ATM, or get more cash by borrowing against a credit card. All of these choices can be dangerous if you do not track them. If you take cash from the ATM and don't record that withdrawal, and then you plan to pay your cell phone bill online, you may find you don't have enough money in your account. Fortunately, there are warning systems you can build in to let you know when your bank balance is below a certain level and overdraft protection on your checking account that you can use to make sure you don't spend more than you have. However, like the athlete who loses strength when he does not continue his training, you must keep using these tools to ensure financial stability.

Developing a good credit score is critical when you are an adult. You may need it to finance a car loan or to get a mortgage loan for a house. Every time you are late with a credit card payment, or don't have enough money for a check you have written, your credit score may be affected. These problems can become serious obstacles standing in the way of things you want to accomplish, so developing and using compensatory systems to help you manage your finances before you become an adult is essential.

SOCIAL RELATIONSHIPS

Some children with ADHD often have difficulty negotiating social situations. You may have trouble handling frustration or controlling your emotions, leading you to have outbursts and making other kids not want to be your friend. If you are in a crowded room with many people and activities, you may get overwhelmed and so distracted that you can't maintain focus on a single person or discussion. Friends don't understand this and so they may walk away from you and turn to someone else who will maintain the conversation with them.

Some people with ADHD may also have difficulty reading social cues. You may not pick up on details such as tone of voice, body language, or someone's posture, which indicate the other person's feelings or mood and so, without meaning to, you act inappropriately. Some of you may also have been diagnosed with a Nonverbal Learning Disorder (NLD) if you had these social problems and also were weaker in math, spelling, and motor coordination. To address these problems, you may have participated in social skill groups where you learned to read these social cues just like you learned to take notes or study for tests. Those skills need to continue to be part of your repertoire as you get older. In the workplace, poor social skills can affect your work performance because you may not read your coworker's nonverbal cues during a meeting or may not realize that your boss is becoming annoyed by something you are doing.

Depending on what you choose as a career, you may be in a position of interacting with others, perhaps supervising them or at least hoping to become friends with them. Although adults may be more tolerant of some of these social difficulties, you still need to continue using all of the strategies and skills you learned earlier. Often, because adult interactions are even more complex, you will need to learn some new skills to navigate the adult world and do well professionally and socially.

COMORBIDITY

Because we are talking about some of the more negative aspects of having ADHD, we thought we would get something else out of the way: comorbidity.

Comorbidity: A fancy way of saying "other problems that tend to go with a particular problem."

There are many comorbid conditions that seem to go along with a diagnosis of ADHD and you may be experiencing one or more of these comorbid problems. Some authors (Reiff & Tippins, 2004) believe that as many as one half to two thirds of children with ADHD are also experiencing one or more other conditions.

In a long-term study of children between the ages of 7 and 9, 34% were found to have experienced anxiety within the preceding year, and 4% were found to have experienced depression within the year prior to the study (MTA Cooperative Group, 1999). But in another study performed with individuals between the ages of 9 and 16, many more students with ADHD, 48% of them, experienced symptoms of depression (Bird & Gould, 1993). What these studies suggest is that depression is often not diagnosed until kids get older (Brown, 2005). These comorbidities are often missed for several years because many of the symptoms look just like the symptoms of ADHD. Let's look at some of the most common comorbidities one at a time.

ANXIETY

Various studies have indicated that adolescents with ADHD are about three times as likely to experience anxiety as those without ADHD (Gregg, 2009). It may have been hard for others to recognize your anxiety because these feelings are going on inside you and others don't see them easily. It is only when the anxiety becomes worse and you are very irritable, you stop eating, or have trouble sleeping that your parents or doctor may realize that there are problems with anxiety. If you are just restless or stressed, they may assume it is due to your ADHD.

"I was so frustrated because even though I knew the medication I was taking helped me to focus and get my work done, I kept getting more and more stressed when I took it. I felt like I had to choose between feeling OK but being totally distracted or being able to get my work done and getting more and more worried and upset."

—Evan, age 18

There have been studies that indicate that some medications used for ADHD will increase anxiety in some students; this is not always the case. But often medication has to be changed or adjusted once anxiety is diagnosed.

DEPRESSION

Estimates are that about 30% of children and teens with ADHD develop symptoms of depression (Parker, 2002). We know that everyone feels discouraged or "down" some of the time. If you are struggling with schoolwork, or having trouble with friends, you are even more likely to feel unhappy and your self-esteem may suffer. This may or may not be an indication of depression. If the feelings are based on some experiences you are having and the feelings go away when those situations change, it's likely not depression but a byproduct of difficulties associated with ADHD. For example, if you're upset because you're always getting bad grades in school and then you start getting some accommodations in school and tutoring so your grades improve and you feel better, then you are probably not struggling with depression, but with an understandable reaction to a difficult situation. However, if you're not sleeping or eating well, if you're tired, feel badly about yourself, or are no longer interested in things you used to like, then you need to talk to your parents, your doctor, or your school counselor to see if you are experiencing some depression in addition to ADHD.

OTHER BEHAVIOR PROBLEMS

In addition to anxiety and depression, sometimes ADHD is seen alongside other behavior problems. Certain kids with ADHD seem to get into trouble all of the time. They break rules, take things that don't belong to them, destroy property, or bully other children. This may not be just because they have greater difficulty controlling their impulses than most kids do. Many kids with ADHD are mischievous, but most of them don't get into the kind of trouble that can get them suspended from school or have them break the law. Kids who do have more serious behavior problems are often called "oppositional" or are said to have conduct problems in addition to their ADHD. Kids with these problems can learn to control their behavior with the right kind of structure and treatment.

LEARNING DISABILITIES

It is difficult to really know how often ADHD occurs with learning disabilities (LD) because there are so many different definitions of LD. In a study conducted in 2000, Rosemary Tannock and Thomas Brown reported that all three types of learning disabilities (reading, writing, math) occur two to three times as frequently in children with ADHD compared to children without ADHD. Some researchers (Brown, 2005; Swanson & Saez, 2003) said that this is because if you have ADHD, you often have weaker working memory and executive functioning skills, and these are needed for effective learning, but not everyone holds this belief.

The most common form of LD associated with ADHD is seen in problems with output. If you have difficulties organizing what you want to say and getting it on paper, and then finishing it on time, that is often considered an output or production problem. This kind of problem may be considered a learning disability or a problem associated with the organizational aspects of executive functioning. Other problems associated with executive functioning that we have already discussed (such as time management and prioritizing) are sometimes also labeled as learning disabilities. The good news is that these difficulties can sometimes help you qualify for a 504 Plan or IEP in school so you can receive accommodations and be more successful academically. We will discuss these school accommodations in Chapter 6.

THE GIFT OF ADHD?

Some people say that having ADHD can be a "gift" (Honos-Webb, 2005). These gifts include greater creativity, being able to think outside of the box, and being more emotionally expressive. Having a higher energy level can be an asset when it is focused and directed. We have talked to adults who say ADHD allows them to accomplish more. However, we have yet to find a teenager who was happy about having ADHD.

WHERE IS JAKE?

Jake has many of the symptoms of executive functioning and learning disabilities that accompany his ADHD. He is very bright and although his ADHD was diagnosed when he was young, it was not until middle school that problems were noticed. Once he had to juggle seven teachers and the different assignments and manage his time on his own, his grades started declining. He wouldn't know that he had a test on Friday and would be totally unprepared when it came up. He didn't plan ahead so he was not able to get long-term projects finished on time. His school put additional goals and accommodations in his IEP to help him with these issues. He began to meet with the resource teacher every day, and she helped him schedule his assignments so they were done on time. He learned that he had to check his notes with another student to be sure he was not missing important information like the date of an upcoming test.

Although Jake's grades improved by eighth grade, he found that high school was even more demanding and he had to develop new strategies. Even though Jake is very bright, when he goes on to college and pursues a career he will continually have to be aware of these issues and develop new strategies to accommodate the increased demands and expectations imposed in a college setting.

WHERE IS ABBY?

The inattentive symptoms of Abby's ADHD became more severe in middle school. She also experienced significant anxiety, partly due to the ADHD, but she was also diagnosed as having anxiety as a comorbid condition. In other words, even if Abby did not have ADHD, she would still be experiencing anxiety. This became a "double whammy" for her because the stress of her anxiety made it even more difficult for her to focus.

Abby got some help initially by talking to her counselor at school and then her parents found a private therapist for her to talk to. When Abby was in middle school, her doctor changed her ADHD medication to one that could also help her with her symptoms of anxiety. The combination of the medication and the counseling helped Abby deal with the combined issues of ADHD and anxiety. As she gets older, Abby may need to continue medication or she may find that developing some strategies (e.g., relaxation techniques, self-talk) may be helpful enough without the medication.

Highlights and Recap

➤ For the majority of students with ADHD, many symptoms continue as you become an adult.

➤ Aspects of executive functioning include:
- ☞ getting started on tasks (activation),
- ☞ time management, and
- ☞ prioritizing.

➤ Other sources of difficulties may arise if you also have a comorbid condition such as:
- ☞ anxiety,
- ☞ depression, and
- ☞ learning disabilities.

➤ If you keep using the strategies you will learn in this book, take medication if it is helpful, and work with a coach if you need one, you can be happy and successful even with ADHD, but it is important not to slack off because if you do, you most likely will have problems that will interfere with your success.

CHAPTER 5

WHAT DOES TREATMENT LOOK LIKE?

"Five minutes! Zounds! I have been five minutes too late all my lifetime!"

—Hannah Cowley

L et's pretend that you are one of the top-ranked lacrosse players in your school. What would you do if your coach told you that to maintain your top status you had to make some changes? He tells you that you have to change your diet (no more midnight pizza binges), get more sleep, and start taking a multivitamin to ensure that your brain and muscles are getting all of the right nutrients. It's unlikely that you would tell him to take a hike and stick to your old habits, right? Well, the same thing is true for you and your ADHD—even more so if you actually are one of the top-ranked lacrosse players in your school. Although ADHD is potentially a lifelong condition that affects you in many ways, it doesn't mean there is nothing you can do about it. In this chapter, we are going to talk about how to treat your ADHD. We will cover three major components of ADHD treatment. Research shows that if you do all three, it is much less likely that your ADHD will create major negative consequences for you now, as well as later in your life. These components include medication, changing your behavior and environment, and using accommodations and advocating for yourself.

Ways to treat ADHD:
- → medication,
- → changing behavior and environment, and
- → using accommodations and advocating for yourself.

The key point here is that you have to do all three of these things to make a major impact on your ADHD. Although doing one or two will help, the combination of all three is where success is truly found. Let's take a closer look at these treatment components.

MEDICATION: A VALUABLE INGREDIENT, BUT NOT THE WHOLE ENCHILADA

Way back in the 1990s, in the early days of video games before there were websites devoted to "cheat codes," there was a device called a "Game Genie." This device plugged into your game console. When you plugged the game cartridge into the Game Genie, it helped you learn the game by giving you extra lives and access to advanced weapons. These were valuable tools that helped kids learn how to play the game and advance to new levels.

You can look at medication like a Game Genie. Just like the Game Genie didn't substitute for skill—you still had to beat the boss at the end of each level—medication does not "cure" your ADHD. It doesn't make you smarter and it doesn't do your algebra for you. However, ADHD medication can make it much easier for you to sit still in class and pay attention to the algebra lesson. Similarly, medication won't make you remember to turn in your homework, but it can slow your mind down so you can come up with a system for remembering to turn in your homework.

Now if you are like many of the students we work with, you might be thinking, "but I don't want to put anything in my body that's going to change me." Not to worry. Medication does not change who you are or how you feel. Like we said, it is simply a tool to help you manage your ADHD better. Think of it this way: If you were nearsighted and couldn't see road signs when you were driving, you wouldn't give up driving because you didn't want to wear glasses, would you? Just like glasses help your eyes see better, medication can help your brain focus better and your body be at rest.

Doctors have been prescribing medication to treat ADHD for more than 30 years (Barkley, 2006). There are many ADHD medications and ways of administering them (e.g., pills, capsules, liquids, even a skin patch). We know what the medication helps and what side effects it can produce. There are thousands of studies about ADHD medication that document its effectiveness. For example, studies have shown that your age, gender, and even the time of day you take the medication can influence its effectiveness.

One of the first medicines used to treat ADHD was called Ritalin. It is from a class of drugs called stimulants. We know what you're thinking—"I'm already hyper enough, why would I want to put something in my body that speeds me up more?" Although it sounds contradictory, we do know that these drugs can significantly improve ADHD symptoms in the majority of people who take them (Barkley, 2006). Although Ritalin is very effective at managing the symptoms of ADHD, it does not work for everyone and it has one major drawback—it stays in the body for such a short time that it needs to be taken several times a day to remain effective. That could be very inconvenient for an active student in school. So scientists began experimenting with the Ritalin molecule and have come up with longer acting versions of it (e.g., Ritalin LA—the LA stands for Long Acting). Another popular stimulant, Adderall, has a capsule version called Adderall XR20, which releases 10 milligrams of the drug immediately and 10 milligrams 4 hours later. The obvious advantage of these long-acting forms is that you don't need a mid-day dose during school. Researchers also discovered other stimulants that are just as effective as Ritalin, but last longer. Ritalin LA and these other drugs have the advantage of needing to be taken just once in the morning, but remain effective throughout the school day and late into the afternoon (so that homework can be done). Table 1 includes a list of some of the drugs commonly used to treat ADHD.

Stimulant drugs are by far the most popular (and some say most effective) medicines used to treat ADHD. But like all medicines, they can have side effects. The most common side effects are decreased appetite and sleep problems (National Institute of Mental Health, n.d.). Because these drugs stay in the body longer, they can still be effective when it's time to turn your brain off and go to sleep. If this happens to you, talk to your doctor. He or she may be able to change your dosage (or change the drug) so that it does not affect your sleep.

A far less common, but just as serious side effect that can sometimes occur with these drugs is a change in personality. A few kids report that they become less lively and expressive when they take their medicine. Although not life-threatening, this "flattening" of personality can be very upsetting. Should you experience this or any other side effect from taking a stimulant medication, tell your parents and doctor. A change in dose or choice of medication could make a big difference.

Although stimulants are the most popular medicines used to treat ADHD, they are not the only class of drugs available. Called "nonstimulants," these other drugs work in a different way, but

Table 1
Medications for ADHD

Stimulants	Nonstimulants
Adderall	Strattera
Concerta	Intuniv
Daytrana	Wellbutrin
Dexedrine	
Focalin	
Metadate	
Ritalin	
Vyvanse	

can be just as effective. The two most common nonstimulant drugs used to treat ADHD are Strattera and a relatively new drug called Intuniv. One disadvantage of these medicines is that they can take several weeks before they start working.

If you and your parents decide to try medicine to treat your ADHD, you may have to visit your physician, who will prescribe the best drug and dosage for you. Sometimes, instead of your regular doctor, your parents might take you to see a psychiatrist to get the prescription. Psychiatrists are specialists who deal only with problems in daily functioning. These doctors know a lot about this one area, while your regular doctor has to know a little bit about a lot of areas because he or she treats your whole well-being. Whichever kind of doctor you meet with, it's important that you tell him or her how the medicine makes you feel and whether or not you think it is helping you.

CHANGING BEHAVIOR AND STRUCTURE

No matter what medicine you are taking, you know by now that it is not going to solve all of the problems that can come with having ADHD. Just like the Game Genie didn't substitute for skills and practice, medicine doesn't substitute for making changes in your behavior that will help you cope with your symptoms.

Besides your pediatrician or psychiatrist, another professional you may be working with is a therapist. He or she may be a psychologist, social worker, or counselor, and he or she probably works with you as well as with your parents. Your therapist's job is to educate you and your parents about ADHD and advise you about what changes you need to make to your home and school environments so that you can manage your ADHD symptoms better. For example, the therapist may suggest that your parents have you stick to a regular schedule. Knowing what to expect and when to expect it can help you manage your attention. Let's say that your family had no regular dinner schedule. If you are taking one of the long-acting stimulants, you may need to do your homework before it wears off so that you can concentrate better. But if dinner is at 5 o'clock some nights and 7 o'clock other nights and you like to do your homework after dinner, your medication might wear off before you get to your homework!

Therapists may suggest many other things as well. They might help you set up a special study space. Or they may help you figure out how to get more exercise or better sleep because studies show that rest and certain exercises can improve overall well-being as well as attention (Ratey & Hagerman, 2008). A therapist can also help you deal with your feelings about ADHD. Many kids we have worked with eventually ask themselves, "Why me? Why do I have to have ADHD?" A trained therapist can help you put your ADHD in perspective and realize that you have many other strengths and good qualities besides the fact that you can't pay attention.

Because many individuals with ADHD have trouble getting along with their peers, a therapist can help you learn how to recognize when your hyperactivity is beginning to bother others so you can alter your behavior before it causes problems with your friends. For example, if you always get excited when you have a sleepover, a therapist can teach you relaxation strategies that you can use before your friend comes over so you don't act like a spaz when she gets to your house. Regardless of what your therapist suggests, it is important that you keep an open mind about therapy and try something before deciding that it won't work.

Another person your parents may bring you to is an ADHD coach. Just like a sports coach can help you to improve your game, an ADHD coach can help you improve the quality of your school-work. Coaches teach methods of organization and study skills, as well as help students find ways to become more motivated about schoolwork. Coaches usually meet with their students once or twice a week to go over assignments and provide feedback. They also may schedule phone or e-mail check-ins to provide additional support or encouragement. A coach can be especially useful if you and your parents often argue about homework. The coach can be an objective third party and many students find it easier to follow the advice of a coach than their parents.

> "I hated the idea of having to work with a tutor at first, but now it's OK because he really helps me."
>
> —Michael, age 13

SELF-ADVOCACY AND ACCOMMODATIONS

This can often be the hardest part of a treatment plan for people with ADHD. It is one thing to accept help, like taking medication or advice from a therapist, but self-advocacy involves your looking ahead and preventing problems before they happen. Your parents can take you to the best doctor and she can prescribe the perfect medication for you, but you still have to remember to take it. Your therapist or coach can devise the best study schedule for you, but you still have to implement it. Get the picture yet? You are the most important part of your treatment plan because you have to want to improve things and be willing to try things if they are going to work.

So how can you self-advocate? The first thing is to not be embarrassed about your ADHD. Remember, you are in some pretty good company

> "I wouldn't use my accommodations in school because I didn't want my friends to think I was stupid."
>
> —Allyson, age 15

(like Michael Phelps) and millions of kids in the U.S. have the same type of problems that you do.

We can't reiterate this enough: Having ADHD does not make you stupid. There's no reason to be embarrassed about your ADHD the way Allyson was—lots of kids get different accommodations in school to help them with everything from needing extra time on tests, to going to the nurse's office, to use their inhalers so they can breathe better. Don't be shy about letting your teachers, coaches, boss, or friends know what you are struggling with. Some of them may share their struggles with you too! Here are some specific strategies that you can employ in your life right now.

In School

➤ Inform your teachers of your needs early in the semester. Most will be receptive to your needs if alerted to them before there is a problem.

➤ Don't hesitate to question teachers if you do not understand something. It is important not to let this go, as the next class is apt to build upon the class before.

➤ Ask for examples, applications, or rephrasing, rather than repetition.

➤ Participate in class discussions. This can bring up your grade if you have a problem with a test or other assignments. Remember, asking questions is part of participation.

➤ If possible, join or create a study group to discuss and review material.

At Home

➤ Ask your parents to give you a written list of chores that you can hang up in your room rather than having them just tell you what they want you to do.

➤ When your parents are giving you instructions, try to maintain eye contact with them.

➤ If you want to work more independently at home, start by telling your parents that you will check in every 20 minutes to show them what you have accomplished. Later, that time period can be extended as you prove you can do it.

➤ Establish your own study periods by using your calendar, timers, and other tools.

With Your Friends

➤ Make a private agreement with your best friend to signal you when you are getting too "hyped up" with your friends.

➤ When you schedule activities with your friends, make sure you check your schedule so you don't forget to meet them. Set alarms so that you are on time.

➤ When you are going to meet friends at the mall or other place, leave 10 minutes early so you aren't late.

➤ When angry or upset with a friend, wait at least one hour before you respond to a text or e-mail. This will give you time to calm down and think so you don't say something you might regret.

WHERE IS JAKE?

Soon after Jake was diagnosed with ADHD, his parents brought him to his pediatrician who evaluated him for medication. The doctor prescribed Ritalin for Jake. Although his teacher reported that it seemed to help a little, by early afternoon Jake was having trouble staying focused again. So Jake's doctor changed his prescription to the long-acting form of Ritalin (Ritalin LA) and this seemed to do the trick. Although Jake was now doing better in school, his parents still found his behavior to be challenging at home. To address these issues, Jake's parents consulted with a psychologist who gave them some strategies to implement at home. These strategies seemed to work for several years, but when Jake got to eighth grade, his grades started to decline. He had a hard time keeping track of his assignments and couldn't always get his homework done. Jake's parents hired a coach for Jake who helped him learn how to manage his schoolwork more effectively. Now that Jake is in ninth grade, he still takes his medication and meets with his coach once a week.

WHERE IS ABBY?

Because Abby has the inattentive type of ADHD, it took her parents and teachers a little longer to identify her problems. Once she was diagnosed, her parents hired a tutor who helped Abby and her parents develop a home organization system and schedule so that Abby could better manage her school and home responsibilities. The tutor also introduced Abby to the Skoach calendar (see http://www.skoach.com) so she could keep track of homework, class assignments, projects, and her social activities. With this system in place, Abby stopped missing assignments and was much less often late for dates with her friends. As she entered middle school and her comorbid anxiety increased, Abby's parents brought her to a therapist who taught Abby relaxation strategies to reduce her anxiety and provided her with an outlet to talk about her concerns. Additionally, Abby's therapist taught her how to advocate for herself with her teachers so that she could receive the accommodations her 504 Plan entitled her to. Abby also started taking medication to decrease her distractibility when she entered middle school. As her concentration improved, so did Abby's grades. These better grades, along with her therapist's help, reduced her anxiety so that Abby could enjoy her free time more and not worry so much about things.

Highlights and Recap

➤ There are three components to ADHD treatment: medication, changing structure and behavior, and self-advocacy and accommodations.

➤ Although any one or two of these can be effective, doing all three components provides the greatest impact to minimize the negative affects your ADHD will have on your life.

➤ Although medication is not a cure-all, it can be a powerful tool in reducing ADHD symptoms.

➤ There are two classes of ADHD medications: stimulants (e.g., Ritalin) and nonstimulants (e.g., Strattera).

➤ Family doctors or psychiatrists can prescribe ADHD medications.

➤ Therapists, counselors, and tutors/coaches can provide information and strategies to change your behavior and structure at home or school to manage your ADHD.

➤ Advocating for yourself by letting others know what you need is an important skill for you to learn.

CHAPTER 6

HOW DO I GET HELP AT SCHOOL?

"Something a guy never wants to hear,
'Tim, the school called!'"

—Tim Allen

aving ADHD affects how most students do in school at some point, but it doesn't affect everyone the same way or at the same time. Some of you may have breezed through the early school years before anyone even noticed you had ADHD. For others, when you were 3–4 years old, you may have been told that you were a behavior problem and just couldn't get along with other kids. At the time, no one realized this was part of your ADHD. Still some others of you may have been diagnosed just as you were entering kindergarten; your parents talked to your teachers or the principal and they were able to put together a plan that worked for you.

Most kids with ADHD are first diagnosed when they are in elementary school. You may have noticed some problems yourself in first or second grade. For example, even though all of your friends were very active and had trouble sitting still when you were all in preschool and kindergarten, all of a sudden when you entered first or second grade, they were able to settle down but you couldn't.

Your teacher was giving lots of directions and you had trouble remembering them all. You were supposed to finish a certain amount of work independently but you never finished it. Managing recess may have been even more difficult because you were left on your own and the teachers weren't telling you what you should do and when you should do it. Even though you noticed that you had a harder time with some of these things than your friends did, your parents or your doctor may have said you were just developing a little later and you would outgrow these problems, but now you know you really didn't.

> "I don't remember when I was told or if it was explained to me—I just know I had a lot of energy."
>
> —Nick, age 15

But we're sure some of you weren't diagnosed with ADHD while you were in elementary school at all, so no one knew how hard you were working. You may have been managing well enough that no one thought the problems were serious enough to do anything about. Your parents were on your case at home to be sure you finished your homework, and they would remind you again and again to turn in a permission slip or bring home the two coats you left at school, and somehow you managed. You probably heard many people say you were really brighter than your grades showed. And we bet the comment, "You are not working to your potential," sounds pretty familiar, but again, no one did anything really different for you until things became more serious.

For many of you, it wasn't until you reached middle school or maybe even high school, that things began to fall apart. All of a sudden you had to manage six or seven different classes and teachers, each of whom had different teaching styles and expectations. You might have come home very upset, or you were studying longer than your friends and were still failing tests. Eventually, your teachers or parents called for a meeting and people began to notice that things were not working for you.

Regardless of when someone stepped in to help you, specific methods and plans were put in place to give you support and accommodations in school. Let's discuss the four most frequent ways for you to get extra help in school:

➤ informal support,
➤ Response to Intervention (RTI),
➤ 504 Plans, and
➤ Individualized Education Programs (IEP).

The most frequent ways to get help in school include:

→ informal support,
→ Response to Intervention (RTI),
→ 504 Plans, and
→ Individualized Education Programs (IEP).

INFORMAL SUPPORT

In the younger grades, you may have had a few teachers who really understood why you were having trouble and what would be helpful for you. Because you often had the same teacher for most of the day, it was easier for that teacher to give you whatever accommodations you needed. For example, you always sat in the front of class away from a particular student who bothered you, the teacher often came over to your desk to be sure you were on the right track, and she gave you extra time to finish your work if you needed it. Your teacher may also have shortened homework assignments because she knew it was so hard for you to stay focused for a long period of time, especially after a full day in school. In many schools, this is done without any formal plan; the teacher just does what seems to be helpful, and if you were lucky, you might have had teachers like this 2 or 3 years in a row. But then in fourth and fifth grades, you had different teachers for math and for language arts and they didn't always do things the same way, which became a problem.

If you weren't diagnosed earlier, maybe this was the time that the school did some testing or your parents had you see the pediatrician or another professional to help understand what was going on. You found out you had ADHD. You may also have learned, as we discussed in Chapter 4, that in addition to ADHD, you had some other learning issues that made schoolwork even harder for you. That's why you are reading this book.

You should know that not all students with ADHD are considered eligible for the IEP or 504 Plans we are discussing in the sections that follow. If this is your situation, then informal supports may be the only way you can get any help or accommodations at all. That means it is even more important for you to know what you need and to be able to communicate that to your parents, the counselor, or your teachers.

RESPONSE TO INTERVENTION (RTI)

The Individuals with Disabilities Education Act (IDEA) is a United States federal law that provides special services for students to help them succeed in school. It was modified many times and most recently, in 2004, IDEA was changed to include the term "Response to Intervention" as the first step for children who are struggling in school. In many cases, RTI is no different from what your teachers may have been doing informally all along. In 2004, it became formalized and schools are now required to define whatever plans they are using to help you, and to check regularly to see if these plans are working. Although RTI is not specifically designed to help you with your ADHD, many times students with ADHD are grouped along with other students for this kind of planning. Each school does this a little differently.

At first, you may just work with your regular teacher in the classroom, and he may do some extra things to help you. If this isn't enough, then often a specialist (such as a resource teacher, counselor, teacher's aide, or other professional) comes in to provide more help for you—and probably some other students also. If this isn't working and still you're not doing better, the school might decide to do some testing or provide more services. Now maybe you go out of the classroom for some extra one-on-one help or you work in a small group. Often, however, especially for kids with ADHD, these attempts to help you are not really what you need. You are smart and have the skills; you just can't stay focused to get your work done in class. If this is true for you, then your teachers, parents, and school principal may meet to formulate a 504 Plan or IEP for you.

Response to Intervention (RTI): A system that schools use to provide initial support and accommodations to students who are struggling in the classroom.

504 PLAN

What we call a 504 Plan is really based on Section 504 of the Rehabilitation Act passed in 1973 and the American with Disabilities Act of 1990, so it has been around for a long time. This same law can also ensure that you get accommodations in college or in your workplace if you still need them as you get older, so you really want to understand this well. If you have been diagnosed with ADHD and your parents request it, the school must meet to determine if you are eligible for a 504 Plan (Wright & Wright, 2007).

> **504 Plan:** Based on a federal law, 504 Plans provide formal accommodations to struggling students who have a qualifying diagnosis like ADHD.

The 504 Plan does not offer you special support services like working with a reading teacher or speech/language pathologist, but it does provide accommodations for you to be successful in class and on tests. Even though you may need extra support, it may be that you are working with a private tutor, you don't want to be pulled from class, or you don't want to miss taking some electives, making the 504 Plan the best choice for you. To get a 504 Plan, your school must set up a committee to discuss your situation. The 504 committee consists of school personnel (teachers, administrators, and counselors) and your parents; you can join as well.

If the 504 committee agrees that a 504 Plan is appropriate, you can get accommodations—changes that are made for you in the classroom to help you be more successful. If you are easily distracted, you may be assigned a seat in the front of the class or away from the hall or window where there are frequent distractions. If you often forget your books for homework, you may get a second set of books to keep at home. Because you have trouble staying focused and you may work more slowly, you may get a duplicate set of class notes so you have complete, accurate information when you study. You may also get to take tests in a separate room and with extra time so you can focus more easily. We will discuss other accommodations later in this chapter.

The purpose of a 504 Plan is to give you accommodations, not specialized support from the school. The 504 Plan is reviewed every year and accommodations may be added or eliminated, depending on the committee's opinion of what is helping. You and your parents need to provide information to the committee so the school provides the right accommodations for you.

INDIVIDUALIZED EDUCATION PROGRAM (IEP)

As we said, if the informal support or RTI is not helpful and you are still struggling at school, it is not because you have even worse problems. It means that you need something else that the school is not providing. In this case, the school can consider providing you with an Individualized Education Program (IEP). An IEP can start in any grade. Let's look at how IEPs work.

Like RTIs, IEPs also result from the Individuals with Disabilities Education Act (IDEA). It's important for you to know as much as you can about this process so you can advocate for yourself now and as you get older. The school performs an evaluation by collecting historical data from your parents, gets information from your teachers, may administer formal tests (e.g., IQ, achievement tests), and may observe you in one of your classes. An IEP is provided if a student's progress is limited by one of 13 categories (e.g., learning disabilities, speech and language problems). You are eligible for an IEP if the IEP team thinks that your ADHD interferes with your being able to learn in school. If it's just the ADHD that is causing your problems, then the IEP

> Based on federal law, an IEP is a formal plan that provides support, accommodations, and specialized instruction to students who are struggling in school because of a diagnosed problem like ADHD or a learning disability. Unlike 504 Plans, an IEP includes goals and objectives to address the special needs resulting from a disability.

is given under the category of "Other Health Impaired." If you have learning disabilities, speech issues, or some other problem, the school may use a different category. It really doesn't matter too much what category the team uses. From your point of view, it means you are able to get some additional support and accommodations.

Your teachers, school principal, counselor, school psychologist, and your parents meet to discuss whether an IEP is right for you. You may already have met with some of these people for testing. If you are in high school, it is important for you to go to that meeting, or at least part of it. Even if you are in middle school, discuss with your parents if it is a good idea for you to be included in the meeting if you want to be. At the IEP meeting, the team looks at your grades, your parents and teachers discuss your strengths and weaknesses, and then they decide if an IEP is appropriate for you. Because you know yourself better than anyone else, there is a real advantage to your going to the meeting. You can give information to the committee about why you are struggling and tell them what kind of support you think would be helpful.

What are the accommodations and supports you get with an IEP? There are many different accommodations; we're going to discuss some of them later in this chapter. In addition, you get extra support when you have an IEP. For example, you may get help with your reading or writing skills, be taught specific strategies to be more successful on tests, or learn ways to control your impulsivity or your restlessness so you can focus better in class. You may meet with a special teacher or counselor to work on these skills; these meetings are what the school will consider additional support for you. You may see these people daily or only a few times a month, depending on what the team thinks is necessary. Sometimes this extra help involves your being placed in a class with fewer students or additional teachers.

All supports and accommodations are spelled out in the IEP and all of your teachers will receive copies of it. You and your parents will also get a copy of it. It is really important that you know what is on your IEP. Teachers have a lot of students and they may forget about your test accommodations or there may be a substitute teacher on a day you have a test who has never seen your IEP. It is your job to go up to the substitute and inform him or her of the accommodations you need. Some students copy and laminate their accommodations to put in front of their notebook so they always have it with them to show to the teacher if there is any question.

This IEP gets reviewed at least once a year, and more often if needed. Each year, the team decides whether any changes are needed in the IEP. If you think the support and accommodations are really helping you, it is important that you use these accommodations and tell the IEP team you found them useful, so they include them for you again. If there are other changes you think would be helpful, you need to tell the team about them as well. If you are not going to the meeting, then be sure to tell your parents so they can deliver your message.

MOST FREQUENT ACCOMMODATIONS

Accommodations are available under either a 504 Plan or an IEP. They can apply to activities in the classroom, homework assignments, classroom quizzes and exams, and standardized tests in school. You should know that sometimes you can also get similar accommodations for the ACTs or SATs, but the boards that administer these exams make that decision independently. Let's look at these accommodations in terms of the ADHD symptoms we described in Chapter 3. These are accommodations you or your parents can request to be added to your 504 Plan or your IEP. These are only a few examples that could be helpful. Keep in mind that these are written the way they would appear on your IEP—as if they are directed to your teachers.

Managing Time

➤ Give the student a multipage assignment one page at a time; on each page, write the estimated completion time for that page.

➤ Provide extended time on assignments and/or tests.

➤ Adjust workload (in class and for homework) so the student can successfully complete it.

➤ Monitor the student's involvement to assure on-task behavior.

➤ Have the student estimate time for work completion and compare to actual working time.

➤ Provide clear time limits for each section of work with frequent reminders.

➤ Provide the student with a daily schedule (or class schedule) so she knows what needs to be accomplished during that period.

Restlessness

➤ Provide frequent breaks, especially during tests or when extended time is offered.

➤ Provide instruction in an interactive manner (e.g., hands-on activities, discussion groups, work on the computer).

➤ Shorten assignments.

➤ Allow the student to stand by his desk as he is working.

➤ Provide the student with a predetermined nonverbal signal to alert him to his being off task.

➤ Allow the student to work with an appropriate peer to help maintain on-task behavior.

➤ Allow opportunities for movement (e.g., collecting materials, delivering messages to the office, taking bathroom breaks).

➤ Encourage movement (e.g., walking, stretching) during transition times.

Attention to Details

➤ Use colored pens or highlighters to separate information on the page and to emphasize important words in instructions.

➤ Make sure worksheets have lots of "white space" and are not visually crowded.

➤ Check in with the student to clarify directions.

➤ Provide the student with models of appropriately done work to guide his performance.

➤ Teach the student to color code or number steps in directions to assure attention to each one.

➤ Provide proofreading and self-checking tools for the student to use before work is handed in.

Impulsivity

➤ Use a token reward system to help the student decrease impulsivity.

➤ Allow frequent breaks and legitimate movement opportunities.

➤ Use nonverbal signals (e.g., thumb up or down) to indicate when it is appropriate for the student to talk or ask questions.

➤ Provide a list of relaxation strategies for the student to use when needing to focus.

Executive Functioning

➤ Keep the schedule and routines consistent and posted in a readily visible location.

➤ Repeat oral directions; break them into short, manageable chunks; and have the student repeat them before continuing.

➤ Provide a proofreading "checklist" to structure self-checking work before handing it in.

➤ Check assignment book daily to ensure accurate copying of homework assignments.

➤ Provide a duplicate set of books at home if the student often forgets the right materials.

➤ Provide the student with a syllabus so she can preview information before class to help with the remembering of new information.

➤ Allow the student to e-mail or fax completed homework to teacher to be sure it is handed in on time.

WHAT YOU CAN DO TO HELP

There are two major ways you can help in the 504 or IEP process. The first is to learn to advocate for yourself. This means you are the one who learns to ask for accommodations and explain your difficulties to your teachers. This is often not going to be easy for you. Sometimes there are teachers who are easy to talk to. Other times, you really don't want to talk to a teacher outside of class, but you have to develop that skill. Very few students are comfortable doing this before high school and many still find it hard even when they are in high school or college. But no one knows you as well as you do and no one knows what will work for you as well as you do. You are the best spokesperson for yourself in explaining what is hard and what can make it easier. Try it first with your favorite, friendliest teacher and that will make it easier.

The other aspect of advocating for yourself involves your getting familiar with all of the things we discussed in this chapter. If you have a 504 Plan or an IEP, get to know what is in it. The first step, if your school allows it, is to go to the meeting where these plans are discussed so you understand how they work and you can voice your concerns. After that, carry a copy of your plan or your accommodations list with you in your notebook so if a teacher forgets an accommodation, you can remind him about it. Self-advocacy is the first step to success.

The second step is to begin learning some strategies to cope with your weaknesses. The accommodations and support that the school, your parents, and maybe a tutor are providing won't always continue. At some point, you have to handle these issues independently. You should know that you can often continue to get accommodations even in college, but there may be fewer available as you get older. So the best thing is for you to start working on a few right away so you can handle things independently. It may be as simple as using a computer calendar to track assignments, scheduling a break every 20–30 minutes during homework time, or learning to sit in the front of the class even if the teacher does not assign your seat there. These are beginning steps and then you build on them as you go along. We will be discussing some specific strategies you can work on later in this book and ways that technology can help.

WHERE IS JAKE?

Because Jake was always very active and impulsive, an IEP was developed for him in second grade. Primarily, the IEP goals addressed his difficulties with staying on task and finishing his work. Even though he is very smart and knew the material, he often did not get the work done. At first, the teacher kept him in from recess so he would finish but he had even more trouble staying focused if he didn't get some exercise after lunch.

Jake was a whiz in math but he really struggled with spelling and handwriting. By the time he was in fourth grade, his IEP was expanded to include some learning support like teaching him to use the computer so he could do all of his written assignments on the computer. This made a big difference for Jake. He was willing to write more information and he could use the spellchecker to help proofread his work before handing it in.

Although his IEP continued in middle school and high school, by seventh grade, Jake began to feel embarrassed about being the only one in class using the computer so he went back to handwriting and his grades suffered. His teachers and parents encouraged him to use the computer but he didn't want to look different. It wasn't until he got to high school that he realized it was OK to be himself and use the accommodations that were helpful. His grades immediately improved once he began using the computer for writing again.

WHERE IS ABBY?

Abby's grades never showed her true abilities because she always lost credit for incomplete homework and papers not turned in. Try as she might, she just couldn't seem to get it together to have the right papers at the right place at the right time. But her teachers just thought she wasn't trying and no formal accommodations were given to her until eighth grade; then she was given a 504 Plan. She and her parents were told that in addition to her ADHD (and related to it), she had difficulties with executive functioning. Abby felt relieved just knowing there was a label to what she was struggling with—she was not lazy or dumb. There was a legitimate problem that she could work on.

Her 504 Plan allowed her to have a duplicate set of books at home. Her teachers allowed her to e-mail her assignments to them from home so she wasn't penalized for forgetting to bring in completed work. Her grades improved immediately because she always did her homework and now they could see the high quality of her work. Her 504 Plan continued throughout high school.

However, Abby knew that she would not always be allowed this accommodation so she began to work with a coach (a tutor specially focused on strategies for people with executive functioning issues) who helped her figure out ways she could help herself with these problems. Abby saw the coach twice a week at first and then after a while, she just called her when she needed help organizing a research paper or studying for final exams.

Highlights and Recap

➤ There are informal and formal methods for students with ADHD to get help in school. Most often schools start with the informal ones first and then progress to more formal ones if needed. These include:

- ☞ informal support,
- ☞ Response to Intervention (RtI),
- ☞ 504 Plans (accommodations alone), and
- ☞ Individualized Education Programs (IEP; support and accommodations).

➤ A student can help himself the most by getting familiar with his plans and accommodations so he can advocate for himself and by learning and developing tools and strategies to cope with some of his difficulties so he can remain successful when he needs to work independently.

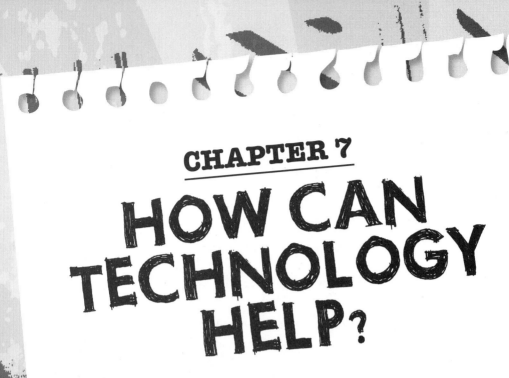

CHAPTER 7
HOW CAN TECHNOLOGY HELP?

"Sometimes a person with ADD feels
as if their mind is moving as fast as
a speeding train."

—Frank Coppola

Believe it or not, there was a time without cell phones, text messaging, or the Internet. The last 20 years have brought profound changes in the way we access information, entertain ourselves, and communicate with each other. Technology has made the world a smaller place where news can spread across the globe in a matter of seconds. Although there are downsides to these technological advances, people with ADHD can use technology to help them cope with some of their difficulties. This chapter is all about technology and tools you can use to help yourself manage your ADHD.

Before we get into the tools, there is something very important that you should remember about using technology. As a character in the Harry Potter books says of technology, "Never trust anything that can think for itself if you can't see where it keeps its brain" (Rowling, 1999, p. 329). We think that what J. K. Rowling means is that you can never rely too much on technology or else you could be in trouble. What if there is a power outage or your fancy gadget breaks—then what good is the technology? We think this is very important to remember. No matter what tools you use to manage your ADHD, you still have to use your brain. Having a fancy alarm clock to remind you to take your meds is going to do no good if you forget to turn it on. So just because technology can help you, don't stop working to improve your own technology—your brain!

There are four ways that technology can help with your ADHD: organization and time management, focusing, memory, and study skills.

ORGANIZATION AND TIME MANAGEMENT

Technology can help you get and stay organized and manage your time better. Most people find that keeping a calendar where they can record assignments and due dates helps to take the burden off of their memory by providing a central place to keep information. It's like having a portable memory storage system so the one in your brain doesn't have to do all of the work.

The simplest form of a calendar is a paper day planner, which can be found at most office supply stores. With this system, you simply write down important events on the proper dates on the paper calendar. The major advantage of this type of system is that it is simple, affordable, and portable. However, as far as technology goes, it is somewhat limited. For this organization system to work, you have to remember to look at it. A day planner can easily be lost or forgotten in the bottom of your backpack. Still, it is a very good and inexpensive system.

A step up the technological ladder is a computer-based calendar. If you have a laptop or easy access to a desktop computer, Microsoft Outlook has a very good calendar built into it. The major advantage of this calendar over a paper one is that you can set alerts to remind you of the events and activities you put in it. For example, let's say that you have a book report due next month. You can set an alert that pops up on your computer screen at a predetermined time to remind you that the book report is due. These reminders save you from having to remember to look ahead at what assignments you have due. Another benefit of electronic calendars is that you can automatically schedule repeating events with a few keystrokes. This means that you don't have to physically enter every weekly appointment with a tutor, for example. Electronic calendars will automatically take one appointment and repeat it every week for as long as you tell it to do so.

Outlook is not the only computer-based calendar available. For example, Google, the Internet search giant, has a very good calendar program that has a really cool feature that will send e-mails or text message alerts to remind you of important information. Imagine that you are out with your friends and that you have forgotten about a paper that's due tomorrow. Wouldn't it be great to get a text message reminding you about the paper so you can get back home to write it?

If you are like most teenagers, your cell phone is an extension of your hand—it's always with you and you are always on it. Most cell phones have calendars built into them and they can be easily used to record your assignments and appointments. In fact, the Google calendar and the iCal program that comes with Apple computers can be synced with your phone so you can look at and add events without having to be at your computer. The major advantage of a phone-based calendar is portability. You can add and change information anytime, anywhere, and it is entirely portable. When you are out with your friends and all of you decide that you want to go to the movies tomorrow, you can immediately check on your phone to see whether or not you have the free time.

If you have a smartphone (e.g., iPhone, Blackberry), there are many apps that can help you keep track of your life. For example, the iPhone app myHomework helps you keep track of classes (great for block scheduling) as well as assignments. Once information is entered, it can be organized by class, assignment, or due date. The main benefit of this app is its portability and ease of use.

For some people, having a place to put events and assignments is all they need to get organized. However, others need assistance with *how* to get organized. If you are someone who needs a more structured organizational system, check out Skoach (http://www.skoach.com). Skoach is a "smart" organizational planning system that incorporates all of the features of an online or smartphone calendar (e.g., text and e-mail alerts, automatically repeating events) with a structured and intuitive system that automatically categorizes events, offers suggested schedules based on events you have entered, and provides templates for how to divide your time into blocks. Although Skoach is an online calendar (like Google), it is fully portable and can be accessed with a smartphone. Because Skoach was designed to help students with ADHD, it can be set up so that a tutor/coach or parent can have access to the calendar to provide support and guidance to the student on how to use it. For example, the coach or parent can access the calendar independently to enter items or check information.

FOCUSING

Remembering assignments and knowing due dates are important, but you still have to sit down and do the work. If you are like many kids with ADHD, staying focused and resisting distractions are not easy for you. How many times have you sat down to do a short, 20-minute assignment only to look at the clock 40 minutes later and realize that you are only halfway done? Luckily there are many tools that you can use to address this problem.

A white noise machine is a great way to screen out other noises so you can more easily stay focused on your work. A white noise machine creates a whooshing sound that makes just enough background noise to mask any other distracting sounds (e.g., traffic noises, your sister's stereo). You can buy these machines online (try Googling "soundscreen") or at many specialty stores like Brookstone. Sometimes white noise machines are built into other devices like alarm clocks. High-end machines offer many sound options besides white noise. You can listen to the sound of the ocean, a babbling brook, or rain shower. You can also make your own white noise machine with a small fan or by tuning in static on a radio.

A great way to stay focused while reading is to listen to books on tape. Listening to a book while reading it helps you pay attention by providing a multisensory experience. Having both your eyes and ears engaged simultaneously while reading decreases the likelihood that you will get distracted by either some external noise or sight or by your own thoughts. Incidentally, this multisensory exposure also improves your memory for the information you are reading. Many novels are now available for download from iTunes or other similar services (e.g., the Amazon Kindle). Your parents can also sign you up with a service like Bookshare (http://www.bookshare.org), which is an online warehouse of books that can be downloaded to your computer. You then use a screen reader program (Bookshare offers a free version of one with membership) that reads the book out loud as you follow along.

A more sophisticated type of text reader is called Kurzweil 3000 by Kurzweil Educational Systems (http://www.kurzweiledu.com). The Kurzweil 3000 is a software program that allows you to scan or download books onto your computer. The program then reads the material aloud as you follow along on the screen. Kurzweil has many great features. For example, you can choose the type of voice (e.g., male, female), change the rate at which the text is read, and highlight text while it is being read aloud. The highlighting feature is useful because it helps you maintain your focus on the text by providing a visual cue. The Kurzweil is also great for completing worksheets because the worksheet can be scanned into your computer and you can type answers directly onto the screen version of the worksheet. The Kurzweil will read both the questions and your typewritten answers. Once you finish the worksheet, you simply print it out and turn it in. Another great feature of the Kurzweil is virtual sticky notes. This feature allows you to attach a note to the text as you are reading. For example, if you come across a passage in a book that would make a great example for your book report, you can attach a virtual sticky note to that passage as a reminder.

Some kids with ADHD can still get distracted even if there is nothing in the environment grabbing their attention. If you often get distracted by your own thoughts, then the following tools are for you. Alarms and timers are a great way to keep on track when studying because they provide an external cue to let you know how much time has passed. Let's take the example we used earlier in the chapter about spending 40 minutes on a 20-minute assignment. Setting a timer and then checking it often as you work can provide you feedback about how much time you are actually spending on the assignment. A simple egg timer will do the trick—it's not very sophisticated technologically, but it gets the job done. In fact, the old-fashioned egg timers with a dial are better than digital ones because the ticking provides an auditory cue along with the visual one. For those of you who are more visual, you can purchase a timer that counts down with a red face as time goes by—the smaller the red face becomes, the less time you have. These kind of timers can be purchased on the Internet (see http://www.eadhd.com or http://www.leapsandbounds.com). Additionally, the iPhone has an application called Time Timer that turns your phone into one of these visual timers.

MEMORY

If you are like many kids with ADHD, you forget a lot of things. How many times have you heard your mom say something like "Don't forget to take your medication!" or "Did you take out the garbage like I asked you to do?" If remembering things is hard for you, there are a number of aids available that can help. If you are using one of the calendars that we talked about, you can set alerts to remind you of important activities like chores, appointments, or medication times. However, what if you are not at your computer to receive the alert? Setting an alert on your cell phone is also a good way to remember things, but what if you don't have your phone with you or it's charging when the alert goes off? The WatchMinder2 (available at http://www.watchminder.com) is the ultimate portable reminder tool. The WatchMinder2 looks like a sports watch and you wear it like a watch. It can be programmed to vibrate and display messages like "take meds," "do exercises," or anything else you want. Because the WatchMinder2 is worn on your wrist, it works wherever you are. For example, you can set it to remind you when it is time to go home. This works great when you are out with your friends and could easily lose track of time. It can help you keep track of breaks while studying or can be programmed to remind you when it is time to start studying.

STUDY SKILLS

There are two exciting pieces of technology that can really improve your schoolwork. The first is an organizational tool that helps with writing. Inspiration (http://www.inspiration.com) is a computer program designed for middle and high school students to help them develop mind maps, webs, and graphic organizers for writing. Inspiration can also help you organize research for a term paper or project. The really cool thing about the program is that after you have your outline/web, all of the information can be transferred to a word processing program with a few keystrokes. Imagine, no more copying the information—the more detailed you make your outline, the less work you have to do on your paper.

The second great pieces of technology that can really improve your studying are the Pulse or Echo Smartpens by Livescribe (http://www.livescribe.com). The smartpen is used for note taking. It consists of a pen that has a built-in tape recorder and uses special paper that keeps track of what you are writing. As you take notes, the smartpen records what your teacher is saying. Later on, while reviewing your notes, you can touch the pen to a word or phrase and the pen will play back what your teacher was saying at the exact moment you wrote the note. This is really great for students with working memory problems or those who cannot take notes and pay attention to the teacher at the same time. The recordings can be uploaded and saved on your computer so you can reference them later.

WHERE IS JAKE?

Throughout middle school and into high school, Jake continued to struggle with time management. He regularly missed deadlines for assignments and was always losing points for turning in homework late. After trying to use several paper calendars with little success, Jake's parents brought him to an ADHD coach. With this coach's help, Jake learned to use Google Calendar to keep track of his schoolwork. Jake liked this system because his coach could access his calendar to add assignments in case Jake forgot them. Jake also found that listening to books on tape while he read not only improved his focus (so he could finish the book faster), but it also improved his comprehension. Jake learned that using timers helped him stay focused when he was working. He experimented with a digital timer first, but it did not seem to help. However, when his parents bought a visual timer and Jake could see the time period getting smaller and smaller, he was better able to manage his attention and finish his assignments in a reasonable amount of time.

WHERE IS ABBY?

Abby took to technology like a duck to water. When her tutor introduced her to Skoach, she quickly adopted it and began recording all of her homework and appointments in it. Because Abby had a smartphone, she was able to sync her Skoach calendar and phone so she could send herself text message reminders. This really helped reduce the number of late assignments and missed outings with her friends. Abby also found Inspiration to be very helpful with her writing. Her essays and book reports became more organized and she found it easier to write once she had a detailed outline to work from. As she got older, Abby became so good at using her organization system that she no longer needed to work with her tutor.

Highlights and Recap

➤ Technology can help you manage many of your ADHD symptoms if you use it consistently and wisely.

➤ A paper calendar is the easiest and cheapest way to organize your assignments and appointments, but is easy to forget to look at or update.

➤ An electronic calendar like Microsoft Outlook is easy to update and can be programmed to send you text message or e-mail reminders.

➤ Smartphone-based calendars are an even more convenient and portable way to keep track of important information.

➤ Skoach is an online organizational system designed for students with ADHD.

➤ White noise machines, books on tape, timers, visual timers, and the Kurzweil 3000 software program are tools designed to help you maintain focus while you are reading or studying.

➤ Inspiration is a computer-based graphic organizer that helps organize research and writing by providing visual webs and flow charts.

➤ The Livescribe smartpens are note-taking tools that allow you to review important parts of lectures by recording speech as you take notes.

CHAPTER 8

WHAT CAN I DO FOR MYSELF?

"You don't motivate people,
you give them self-knowledge."
—Larry Silver

When you have ADHD and people are constantly telling you to "work harder, " "just stay focused," or "stop being lazy," it is understandable that you may become angry and feel inadequate. As we discussed, having ADHD is not your fault and for that matter, it is not your teacher's fault or your parents' fault. It is how your brain is wired and doesn't have anything to do with intelligence. Many of the students we work with who have ADHD are in fact gifted intellectually or in other areas like sports, art, or knowing how to get along with people. One of your jobs is to recognize your strengths and to realize that for you to succeed you may have to educate people about what ADHD is and what you need. That is why we wrote this book and specifically, this chapter—so you can learn ways to empower yourself and be as successful as you can be.

MANAGING YOUR HOMEWORK

We discussed in Chapter 6 ways to help you stay focused in class and accurately get homework assignments written down. So now that you have written down your homework assignment and brought the right materials home, you want to be able to do it correctly and as quickly as possible. What do you need to do?

PLAN YOUR TIME

Think about what you already know about your learning style. Do you have a hard time staying focused when you read? If so, then do your longer reading assignments first while you are most alert. If reading is easier for you, do your other homework first so you can enjoy the reading when you get to it.

Some of you may prefer to tackle the hardest task and get it out of the way first; others may like to do their favorite subject first because it is the easiest. There is no right or wrong answer to this decision; either approach works. Try each approach for a few days and see which one works best for you. Then follow that strategy on a regular basis.

Long-term assignments take special time management skills. First you want a calendar that allows you to see all of the dates between the initial assignment and the date it is due. Then break the assignment into shorter, more manageable chunks. For example, if you have to write a research project, the steps might be:

➤ Choose a topic.
➤ Identify your resources.
➤ Take notes from the resource materials.
➤ Prepare an outline or use a prewriting tool like Inspiration to organize your material.
➤ Write your first draft.
➤ Edit and prepare your final draft.

Estimate how long it will take you to do each step and enter completion dates for each step on your calendar. Once you have done this, you will know when you have to start the project to have it finished on time. The first or second time you do this, you may need help figuring out how long each step will take. You can get that help from a parent, teacher, tutor, or coach.

To help you in the future, chart how long each step really takes you while you are doing it and record the time elapsed; then you can use this information as a guide for planning your next project.

MANAGE THE ENVIRONMENT

Because you have ADHD, you know that you are easily distracted. Some of you are more distracted by visual things—items on your desk, magazines you want to read, your cell phone, your computer screen with your Facebook homepage staring at you, and so forth. You need to put these things away where you won't see them or work in another room away from these distractions. Working at a desk with many distractions means you will take a lot longer to finish your assignments. Why not turn these devices off when you are working and allow yourself time during your break to check your text messages? Treat this as a reward for having worked hard and resisted distractions during your work period.

Some of you may become more easily distracted by auditory factors. You may have trouble concentrating when there is a lot of noise so you need to find a quiet place to study. If your home is too noisy, go to the library. You might also try wearing earplugs (these can be purchased at most drugstores) to block out the distracting noises. Other students can't concentrate when it is too quiet, so if you are one of these students, playing your iPod may actually block out random noises that bother you. Your parents may have a hard time believing this but you can show them this book! Remember, we are only saying you can listen to music; we are not recommending having the TV on or watching YouTube videos because that really is too distracting.

TAKE BREAKS

Because most students with ADHD find it hard to sit in one place for a long time, you need to schedule breaks. Start with a 5-minute break every half hour. If you find you need longer, increase it to 10 minutes, but no longer, or you will never finish your work. The best way to do this is to use a timer. At the beginning of your work session, set the timer for 25 minutes and then when you start your break, set it for 5 minutes. That way, you will not find yourself getting more and more distracted by working too long at any one time, but you will also be sure your breaks don't go on forever.

During the break, get up and move around. Physical exercise helps concentration so shoot some baskets, ride your bike, run up and down the stairs—do anything that requires moving around. Get yourself a protein snack. With this combination, you will get back to work more easily.

TURN IN YOUR WORK

How frustrated would you be if you did all of your homework, but you don't get credit for it because you left it at home? So the final step before you are finished is to put your homework in your folder where you can find it easily the next day. Stuffing it into your backpack often means you won't be able to find it when you want it. Either set aside a separate section of your binder and label it "completed homework" or put the assignment in the subject section where it belongs so it is there when you open your binder in class. Don't put off this step for the next morning; you will be in a rush and it will not happen. Do it right after you finish your work and then you are truly done.

DIET AND EXERCISE

There are many benefits to a good diet and active lifestyle. You can't turn on the TV or open a magazine without seeing a story or ad about the latest diet craze or exercise program that is going to transform your life. Although we can't speak for the accuracy or effectiveness of any of those claims, there are a few things that you can do with diet and exercise to support yourself and minimize your ADHD symptoms.

One of the most basic things that you can do to help yourself is to eat a balanced diet. With today's fast-paced lifestyle, many teens skimp on nutrition by eating fast food or processed foods that have a lot of carbohydrates (such as Hot Pockets). Carbohydrates like breads, French fries, chips, and juices—really anything that has a lot of sugar or white flour—are an important source of energy. However, too many carbohydrates can lead to spikes in blood sugar followed by a carbohydrate crash. After eating a high carbohydrate meal, our bodies experience a rapid rush of energy that quickly wears off, leaving us feeling tired and fuzzy headed. Because you already struggle with staying alert and focused, this seesaw effect does nothing to help you get through a day of classes.

Instead, try eating balanced meals that contain plenty of protein like lean meats and fish, cheese, yogurt, and other dairy products. Proteins cause a more gradual, but steady rise in blood sugar that prevents the "carbohydrate crash." With a steady flow of energy to your brain, you may find it easier to pay attention. For more information about healthy nutrition, check out the U.S. Department of Agriculture (USDA) website on nutrition (http://mypyramid.gov).

Fish oil has been in the news a lot lately. A good source of Omega-3 fatty acids, fish oil has been found to promote healthy hearts and lower cholesterol, and now some studies indicate that it can improve mental focus. Found naturally in fish like salmon and tuna, Omega-3 supplements are now being taken by people with ADHD to help them improve their attention. (Maybe that is why fish is sometimes called "brain food!") Make sure you talk with your parents or doctor before taking any Omega-3 supplements.

There are many reasons why you should exercise, but one specifically related to ADHD is that vigorous exercise leads to the release of important chemicals in the brain that affect focus and attention. In their 2008 book, *Spark*, Ratey and Hagerman talked about the positive effects of exercise on the brain. The authors said that exercises that involve balance, coordination, and intense concentration (like swimming, ballet, yoga, gymnastics, and martial arts) are especially helpful because they involve both the body and the mind. They suggested that their patients with ADHD use exercise as a tool to help them manage their symptoms. They also stressed that exercise is not a substitute for other treatments such as medication, but that it may mean that a lower dose of medication can be effective.

Because exercise has so many health benefits, we encourage you to get off the couch and get active! Whether you participate in organized sports at school or a yoga class at your local YMCA, or simply swim regularly at your community pool, the important thing is to do some form of exercise on a regular basis. Not only will you alleviate some ADHD symptoms, but you'll reduce stress, improve your cardiovascular system, be less tired, and maintain a healthy weight.

NETWORKING

We told you in Chapter 1 that between 3% and 7% of all children in the U.S. are diagnosed with ADHD. That turns out to be between 2 and 5 million kids. If all of the kids with ADHD in the U.S. lived in the same city, it would be larger than Philadelphia or Chicago. That's a lot of fidgety and distracted people! The point we are trying to make is that you are not alone. There are other kids in your town, neighborhood, school, and maybe even classroom who are also struggling with attention issues. Getting to know other kids with ADHD is a great way of getting support and learning how others manage their ADHD. Some schools offer groups for students with ADHD. In these groups, students learn about their diagnosis, share stories about how ADHD affects them, and learn new strategies for managing symptoms. These groups are kept totally confidential because some kids don't want their friends to know they have ADHD.

Another way to get support from other kids with ADHD is to sign up for online networks. For example, ADHD Aware (http://www.adhdaware.org) is an organization run by and for people with ADHD. It offers groups for boys and girls where they can learn more about ADHD and empower each other. Check out their website to learn more about the Go Girls and Boys on the Go clubs. If there is not a club offered in your area, the website provides information on how to start one of your own.

Online forums or blogs are another good resource for finding other teens with ADHD. vBulletin (accessible by going to http://www.addforums.com) has four forums where young people can chat with each other and post messages about their ADHD experiences. For example, the "Hangout" forum is described as a place for teens with ADHD to hangout and talk about what's on their minds. There is also a forum to talk about homework and school issues and another one that deals with friends and relationship issues.

Finally, ADDvance, a website devoted to providing information to people of all ages who have ADHD, has a page for teens (http://www.addvance.com/help/teens) that provides a lot of helpful tips, articles, and resources.

IS YOUR GLASS HALF FULL OR HALF EMPTY?

Some people just seem to be programmed with a "the glass is half full" attitude. If you are one of these people, then emphasizing your assets and strengths will come more naturally to you. But even if you are a "the glass is half empty" person, you still have many strengths. It is important to identify and recognize these strengths and learn how to emphasize them.

Sit down and make a list of the things you do well and those that you struggle with. You may have trouble with this list. Think of the activities you enjoy. Likely you are involved in activities that tap into your strengths, so listing these things is a good place to begin. For example, when you can choose what to do in your spare time do you get involved in sports? Do you draw? Do you take picture, watch movies, or play music? Excelling in these activities probably means you are stronger visually than verbally.

On the other hand, if you prefer to be interacting with people, reading, or writing stories and poetry, your verbal abilities are your strength. If you still are not sure about your strengths, ask a parent or a good friend where that person sees you as being particularly capable and talented. Once you have created this list of strengths, post it where you can see it.

Like it or not, we also all have weaknesses. So as you are gathering lists of your strengths, you will realize that there are some tasks that are more difficult for you. Think about activities you avoid or put off until the last minute. These are probably areas in which you don't feel confident. Include on this list academic subjects as well as activities you do outside of school. For example, you may play guitar wonderfully by ear but can't read music. This can translate to your learning by listening (you are an auditory learner), but it may also mean that your reading skills are weaker. So you would do well in a class where there is a lot of discussion and interaction; a class where you have to read independently would be harder for you. Once you get the knack of thinking this way, you will be able to identify your strengths and weaknesses pretty accurately.

This information may seem more closely related to learning and school and you may ask why it has anything to do with your ADHD. Even though students with ADHD are often bright, they need to find ways to compensate for their distractibility. Knowing how you learn and what learning environment is best for you will help you identify the settings in which your ADHD is less likely to interfere.

Another way to get this information is to refer back to an evaluation if you have had one. Set up an appointment with the person who did the testing, with your parent or tutor, or with a counselor at school to go over the results. Ask this person to help you understand what all those numbers say about how you learn and your strengths and weaknesses. Many professionals feel that students shouldn't see the actual scores and we usually agree. You don't need to know the specific numbers, you just need to know which ones are higher and which ones are lower to identify your strengths and weaknesses. Based on your test profile, these adults can then help you understand how you process information and how you learn.

For example, you may find out that your memory skills are really strong when you experience something like a trip or a specific event. Under those circumstances you remember all of the details and can recall them easily. On the other hand, when you are trying to memorize dates for a history test or math facts, your memory seems to disappear. In fact, there are different kinds of memory and you may have good memory for meaningful information that you learn experientially; discrete memory for isolated information that makes no sense to you is much more difficult.

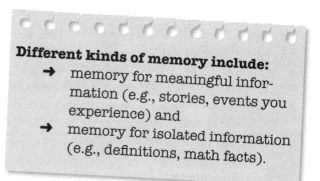

Different kinds of memory include:
→ memory for meaningful information (e.g., stories, events you experience) and
→ memory for isolated information (e.g., definitions, math facts).

Or, if in fact you are a visual learner, you will likely understand a math word problem by drawing a picture that illustrates the problem better than by reading or repeating the words. Information may stick in your brain more easily if you create pictures and images in your mind than if you try to remember individual words. When you read, using different color highlighters will help you pick out important facts. These strategies work for someone whose visual processing is a strength.

On the other hand, if you are a verbal learner, you will benefit from repeating information aloud to yourself as you study so you can hear the words. Study groups where you and others are discussing the topics aloud can help you process and remember the material. Reading really does get the information into your brain.

These are just a few examples of ways you can use information about yourself in a very practical way in school and elsewhere. Combine this with what you discover in Chapter 9 about your ADHD profile to gather as much information as possible about what works for you.

WHERE IS JAKE?

Jake is fortunate to be a natural athlete. He played a different sport each season and this gave him all of the benefits of exercise and offered an outlet for some of his excess energy. It allowed him to get to know teammates who also had ADHD. Even though he distracted his friends in class, they appreciated his humor and energy on the field. They shared medication stories and the horrors of trying to sit still in classes with teachers who didn't understand their need to move around. Jake was the kind of kid who needed frequent breaks during homework time. The most effective thing he could do for himself was to shoot baskets during his breaks. He felt that this cleared his head and allowed him to refocus on his assignments. Because of his athletic successes, Jake was a glass half full kind of person who didn't often let the fact that he had ADHD get him down. Jake's resource teacher and coach helped him realize that, based on his ADHD profile, he did best in classes that provided him with a lot of hands-on activities.

WHERE IS ABBY?

Because Abby was eager to have lots of friends, she found a local chapter of the Go Girls club and was able to share her experience of ADHD with other girls who had similar issues. They helped her develop skills to interact more successfully with girls in school. Abby did not play any team sports, but at her therapist's suggestion, she enrolled in a yoga class. The advantage was that she learned poses and stretches that she could do at home during study breaks. This helped her stay focused during homework time. Abby's tutor introduced her to the WatchMinder2. She programs in her dates with friends, as well as reminders to stay positive and calm on days when she has tests. Unlike Jake, Abby didn't always see the glass as being half full, so she worked with her therapist to develop a list of her strengths and weaknesses. Abby was surprised to see how many assets she had when she focused on them. To empower herself in school, Abby participated in her 504 Plan meetings and made a list of her accommodations that she carried with her to all of her classes.

Highlights and Recap

➤ There are many things you can do for yourself to manage your ADHD symptoms.

➤ Managing your homework involves planning your time effectively, minimizing distractions, maintaining your focus, and developing a system to make sure you get your homework turned in on time.

➤ Eating fewer carbohydrates and more protein provides more energy and eliminates carbohydrate crashes so you can remain focused over a longer time period.

➤ Regular exercise helps to burn off excess energy and promotes the release of healthy chemicals in the brain that increase alertness and focus.

➤ There are numerous resources on the Internet for teens that offer support and helpful information about living with ADHD.

➤ It is important to remain positive.

➤ By identifying your strengths and weaknesses you can learn to maximize your assets and compensate for your weaknesses.

CHAPTER 9

PUTTING IT ALL TOGETHER

"My parents and my former faculty members would be surprised that I'm standing here. While my name appeared on several lists in the Dean's office, none of them was the Dean's list my parents wanted."

—Steve Croft

By now, you have read all of the sections of this book and you understand more about ADHD, how it can affect you, and what you can do to deal with it successfully. Let's spend some time reviewing what you have learned and then we will look at how you can tailor this information specifically to you. In each chapter, you have also been able to follow Jake and Abby as we told you more about their ADHD and how they cope with it. Maybe you see yourself in some of the discussions of Jake and Abby, allowing you to already figure out some things that will be helpful for you.

First, we presented the definitions of ADHD and the current conceptualization with the three categories: ADHD, Predominantly Hyperactive-Impulsive Type; ADHD, Predominantly Inattentive Type; and ADHD, Combined Type. If you have been diagnosed with ADHD, it is important for you to know your specific diagnosis to help you understand the symptoms and the learning style that often goes with each type. You also read that there are research findings that show that ADHD occurs as a result of your biology and genetics; it has nothing to do with your intelligence or motivation. You are probably plenty smart and really want to do well but don't know how to get there. Most individuals with ADHD have the inherited type of ADHD, part of your genetic makeup just like the color of your eyes and hair. There is a much smaller number of people with acquired ADHD resulting from some trauma or injury.

We know that ADHD can affect your relationships with your family and friends, your grades in school, and even your performance in activities you really like such as sports or drama. Specific challenges that go with ADHD often include having trouble staying focused, completing tasks, managing your time, and not interrupting others. Any or all of these problems can affect you at home, at school, or with friends. That includes practically all of the things that matter to you, so unless you get these difficulties under control, you may be feeling upset and frustrated a lot of the time. How can you do things differently to make the situation better?

We have discussed various ways to handle these problems. The first is medication and we put this first because a long-term study done over many years at the National Institutes of Mental Health showed that it is the most effective treatment for ADHD (MTA Cooperative Group, 1999). But even though medication can help, there are many different medications available and you need to work with a specialist to be sure you are taking the best medication for you. Each medication works differently for each person so sometimes you need to try several before finding the right one for you.

In addition to medication, there are many strategies and tools available to help you compensate for some of these issues. Alternative treatments were discussed in Chapter 5 and technology tools were discussed in Chapter 7. Technology offers a wide assortment of computer programs and specialized tools, with new technologies being developed almost every day, so look at one or both of these chapters again if you don't think you have all of the tools you need to help you overcome your difficulties. In addition, some students find working with a tutor or coach very helpful to teach them how to apply some of these strategies and tools to their own situations.

And finally, we talked about the specific formal and informal assistance you can get in school. We presented the requirements for a 504 Plan or an Individualized Education Program (IEP) and talked about the different services available with each one. We presented you with many accommodations that are frequently part of these plans so you can see which would be helpful for you and ask for them when you meet with your teachers and counselors at school.

ESTABLISHING YOUR ATTENTION PROFILE

Just like you establish your Facebook profile by inputting information about yourself, we are going to help you develop your "Attention Profile" by using the information you already know and the information you have read in this book. By answering the questions below, you can define the most troublesome symptoms for yourself and find out the best ways to address them.

Have you been diagnosed with ADHD?

1. If no, speak to your parents and your doctor about whether they think this might be the cause of some of the problems you are having.

2. If yes, is it (check one)

    ____ ADHD, Predominantly Hyperactive-Impulsive Type? Go to #3.

    ____ ADHD, Predominantly Inattentive Type? Go to #4.

    ____ ADHD, Combined Type? Go to #5.

    (If you do not know, check with your parents or doctor to find out.)

3. **If You Have Been Diagnosed With ADHD, Predominantly Hyperactive-Impulsive Type:**

    You are often fidgety, restless, and have a hard time sitting still—your motor is always running. When everyone else is sitting, you may be walking around or at least fidgeting in your seat. Your legs may be jiggling or you may be tapping your pencil continuously and not even be aware of it. If you also have impulsive characteristics, then you may often blurt things out without waiting your turn and interrupt others, you may "leap before you look," make careless mistakes, and get yourself in trouble because you don't stop and think first.

    WHERE CAN THIS CAUSE PROBLEMS? EVERYWHERE

    At home, you may not be able to sit through dinner and you certainly can't stay still at a restaurant where you have to wait longer for food to be served and everyone is taking extra time talking and socializing. If you have brothers or sisters, they may always complain that you are interrupting them when they want to say something. You walk around when you are doing your homework and your parents say you should sit down and concentrate.

    At school, even if you sit in the front of the class, sitting still is hard and other students may say you are disturbing them. Because you are so active, it is hard for you to get your work completed on time, or as a coping tool you may rush through and be the first one finished but make many careless mistakes. Either way, you cannot demonstrate what you really know.

With friends, you may tend to interrupt them. Like Abby, you may try to keep a secret but all of a sudden you blurt it out without even thinking. Your friends don't want to tell you things because this may happen again. You are always moving around and friends may think you are impatient or uninterested but this is not true. You may be the fastest one on a soccer team, but if you don't pay attention as you are running, you will miss the goal.

WHAT TO DO

At Home:

➤ Take a break after school before starting your homework.

➤ Set timers to allow yourself a break during long study periods; be sure to set the timer to limit your break also.

➤ Realize that you may learn better while moving, so memorize history dates while bouncing a basketball or learn vocabulary words by repeating them as you walk around the room.

➤ Because you may be prone to careless mistakes, give yourself time to complete your work, put it aside for a while, and then proofread it again.

In School:

➤ Sit near the front of the room, away from distractions like the hall or windows.

➤ Take a legitimate break that allows you to move, like getting a drink of water or being excused for a bathroom break.

➤ Try to arrange your schedule with the classes requiring the most concentration early in the day.

➤ Try to arrange for hands-on, active classes (e.g., PE, art, science lab, lunch) in between other classes where sitting and listening are required.

With Friends:

➤ Arrange activities that involve movement—set up basketball games or go for a hike or bike ride.

➤ If you know you will be sitting for a long time when you see your friends, get exercise before going so you can stay focused more easily.

4. If You Have Been Diagnosed With ADHD, Predominantly Inattentive Type:

You are often daydreaming or tuning out so you lose focus on what is being said or what you are doing. Therefore, you miss important details and information, or you may be preoccupied and not finish what you are doing before going on to something else. You may often lose things or forget what you were going to do. Managing time can be very difficult.

WHERE CAN THIS CAUSE PROBLEMS? EVERYWHERE

At home, your parents are continuously saying that you are not listening, and in reality, you are not listening because you are thinking about something else. The point is that you are not avoiding them but you don't know how to stop your mind from wandering. You may lose your books, your jacket, and your keys and then everyone is angry, including you. Just getting up in the morning and being ready for school on time is a challenge because you get so easily distracted by other things as you are getting ready. You find yourself running out the door, angry and frustrated and probably late for the bus.

At school, you likely miss directions all of the time because you are thinking about something else. Lucky for you, you have good friends who will help you out but that doesn't make you feel good. Losing things in school is also a problem. How frustrating is it if you have completed your homework and can't find it, or have it but you forget to turn it in so your grades suffer? Staying focused for a long time is very difficult so taking final exams or writing long papers is often a special challenge.

With friends, you may be tuning out while they are talking to you, so you don't hear them and they think you are not interested in being their friend. That is not the case, but they don't realize that. You will often be late for appointments because you either got distracted on the way, or you had to spend extra time finding what you were supposed to bring with you. Your friends get impatient with you if this happens frequently.

WHAT TO DO

At Home:

➤ Keep things organized—use colored folders or boxes for different activities.

➤ Keep your study space distraction free: remove clutter from your desk and put your cell phone and computer in another room. Alternatively, do not do homework in your room; work in the library or other places where there are fewer distractions.

➤ Learn to self-monitor (this may require working with a coach); observe whether you are off task and prompt yourself to get back on track.

In School:

➤ Sit near the front of the room, away from distractions like the hall or windows.

➤ Make eye contact with the teacher/speaker.

➤ Make sure you have phone numbers or e-mail addresses for students in each of your classes if you have to call to clarify an assignment or deadline you may not have heard.

With Friends:

➤ Suggest activities with short time spans and lots of interaction—discussion groups, hands-on activities like art projects or photography, or sports—so you are more easily engaged.

➤ If they are close friends, explain to them that you are an individual with ADHD and although you really care about them, you may sometimes lose focus. Ask them to signal you if they see this.

5. **You Have Been Diagnosed With ADHD, Combined Type:**

You may have been diagnosed with ADHD, Predominantly Hyperactive-Impulsive Type when you were younger but this has changed as you entered middle school and high school. You are experiencing symptoms of being very active and fidgety, you find it hard to sit still, and you may also act impulsively. In addition, you are easily distracted and lose focus on things, and you often find yourself thinking about something else when someone is talking to you or when you should be working or studying. Essentially you have many of the symptoms of both the Hyperactive-Impulsive Type and the Inattentive Type we discussed above.

WHERE CAN THIS CAUSE PROBLEMS? EVERYWHERE

At home, when you were younger, you were into everything. Your parents and caretakers had to be with you all of the time to be sure you did not do something to hurt yourself. As you have gotten older, the hyperactivity has mellowed but you still find that your mind is often racing ahead and you cannot focus on what is in front of you. In your room, you are probably chatting online with your friends and the music is playing while you are supposed to be doing homework. No wonder it seems to take forever!

In school, sometimes you are focusing really well but your body is in motion—you may be walking around or standing by your desk, but you are taking in everything that is being said. Teachers often do not make allowances for you to move around in class; they worry that it interferes with your concentration or disturbs others. If they only realized that it is just the opposite!

At other times, regardless of whether you are standing or sitting, your mind is elsewhere and you have just tuned out. In this case, the teacher has no idea that you are not focused on what is being said because you are sitting perfectly still. However, if you get called on to answer a question, it becomes painfully clear that you were not focusing on the class discussion. You may be very bright but your grades don't show it because you run out of time on tests thinking about something else when you should be finishing the test. Your teachers and your parents are always saying you don't "work to your potential."

With friends, as you have gotten older, it has been more important to be able to tune in socially and pay attention to some of the subtleties like their facial expressions or tone of voice. You used to be popular just because you were a good athlete or always eager to play with your friends, but now that is not enough.

WHAT TO DO

At Home:

➤ Take a break after school before starting homework.

➤ Set timers to allow yourself a break during long study periods; be sure to set the timer to limit your break also.

➤ Realize that you may learn better while moving, so memorize history dates while bouncing a basketball or learn vocabulary words by repeating them as you walk around the room.

➤ Because you may be prone to careless mistakes, give yourself time to complete your work, put it aside for a while, and then proofread it again.

➤ Keep things organized—use colored folders or boxes for different activities.

➤ Keep your study space distraction free: Remove clutter from your desk and put your cell phone and computer in another room. Alternatively, do not do homework in your room; work in the library or other places where there are fewer distractions.

➤ Learn to self-monitor (this may require working with a coach); observe whether you are off task and prompt yourself to get back on track.

In School:

➤ Sit near the front of the room, away from distractions like the hall or windows.

➤ Take a legitimate break that allows you to move, like getting a drink of water or being excused for a bathroom break.

➤ Try to arrange your schedule with the classes requiring the most concentration early in the day.

➤ Try to arrange for hands-on, active classes (e.g., PE, art, science lab, lunch) in between other classes where sitting and listening are required.

➤ Make eye contact with the teacher/speaker.

➤ Make sure you have phone numbers or e-mail addresses for students in each of your classes if you have to call to clarify an assignment or deadline you may not have heard.

With Friends:

➤ Arrange activities that involve movement—set up a basketball game or go for a hike or bike ride.

➤ If you know you will be sitting for a long time when you see your friends, get exercise before going so you can stay focused more easily.

➤ Suggest activities with short time spans and lots of interaction—discussion groups, hands-on activities like art projects or photography, or sports—so you are more easily engaged.

➤ If they are close friends, explain to them that you are an individual with ADHD and although you really care about them, you may sometimes lose focus. Ask them to signal you if they see this.

In addition to the specific strategies spelled out above for your particular type of ADHD, here are some more universal tools that can help all individuals with ADHD.

At Home:

➤ Use watches with alarms to alert you to appointment times.

➤ Create a weekly and monthly schedule with all activities, appointments, and set times for homework; monitor each week and revise as needed. There are calendars available on the computer particularly designed for this (e.g., Microsoft Outlook, iCal, Google Calendar). On a weekly basis, prioritize items by assigning numbers to them and do the ones with the highest priority first whether you like them or not.

➤ Preview material the night before or over the previous weekend so the new information discussed in class makes sense to you and you are more likely to stay focused and remember the material.

➤ Eat protein with every meal; research shows this increases concentration.

➤ If you are taking medication and you notice it is not as effective as it once was, make an appointment to speak to your doctor. Dosages often have to be changed as you get older and gain in weight or height.

In School:

➤ By high school, if not before, attend all 504 Plan or IEP meetings about your program so you can explain what works and what doesn't work to those at the meeting and hear the teachers' comments.

➤ If you have an IEP or 504 Plan, make a laminated copy and put it in your notebook or assignment book (whatever you take to all classes). Be sure you know what is in those plans so you can remind teachers if necessary.

➤ Organize your locker: Purchase shelves specifically made to organize lockers and put all books needed in the morning on the top shelf and all books needed in the afternoon on the bottom shelf. Place all necessary tools—calculator, pencil, pens, highlighters, sticky notes, and your assignment book—in a single clear plastic bag that can be taken with you in both the morning and afternoon. Post your schedule on the locker door. If it is helpful, color code your books; for example, cover all morning books in red and all afternoon books in blue.

➤ Seek extra time for tests and, if necessary, take tests in a separate room where there are few distractions. You can also request that you take only one exam per day if it is very difficult for you to remain focused over two lengthy exams.

➤ Ask for a duplicate set of books at home if you frequently forget the right texts to complete your homework.

With Friends:

➤ When it is comfortable, tell a few close friends that you have ADHD. It is nothing to be embarrassed about. Do people who wear glasses feel they have to apologize for wearing them? When your friends know, you can ask them to tell you if you are moving too much or being distracted, so that you can get immediate feedback and become more aware of your problem areas.

➤ Read other books about ADHD or go on the web to read articles and become familiar with the latest research and information. Some suggestions are listed in the Resources section of this book.

Highlights and Recap

As you have read this book, you have followed the stories of Jake and Abby as they have learned about their ADHD and how to manage it. Now it's time to look at where *you* are. You now have a better understanding of ADHD and the fact it is a biologically based condition that does not define you. Although there are hurdles for you to overcome and strategies that you must put in place to manage your symptoms, you can accomplish any goal you seek. Although you know the symptoms don't disappear as you get older, you have a head start because you have identified your problems and are already addressing them. The blank Attention Profile that follows this chapter can help you decide which strategies you can use to take control of your ADHD. We can't promise that everything in high school, or college, or your career will be easy, but you now have tools to use to help you succeed academically, personally, socially, and in the workplace. There is a community of successful adults with ADHD (remember Michael Phelps) and you can be one of them.

We have also provided the resources on the following pages for you to check out and hopefully find even more strategies and techniques that will be helpful. If you have found the information in this book helpful, tell us by visiting our Facebook page at http://tinyurl.com/spodakstefano. Best wishes as you work to take control of your ADHD!

Your Attention Profile

Have you been diagnosed with ADHD?
If no, speak to your parents and your doctor about whether they think this might be the cause of some of the problems you are having.

If yes, it is (check one)

____ ADHD, Predominantly Hyperactive-Impulsive Type

____ ADHD, Predominantly Inattentive Type

____ ADHD, Combined Type

(If you do not know, check with your parents or doctor to find out.)

STRATEGIES I CAN USE:

At Home:

➤ _____

_____

_____

_____

➤ _____

_____

_____

_____

➤ _____

_____

_____

_____

➤ _____

_____

_____

_____

In School:

➤ _____

_____

_____

_____

_____

➤ _____

_____

_____

_____

_____

➤ _____

_____

_____

_____

_____

➤ _____

_____

_____

_____

_____

➤ _____

_____

_____

_____

_____

With Friends:

➤ _____
_____
_____
_____
_____

➤ _____
_____
_____
_____
_____

➤ _____
_____
_____
_____
_____

➤ _____
_____
_____
_____
_____

➤ _____
_____
_____
_____

RESOURCES

BOOKS FOR PARENTS

Attention-Deficit Hyperactivity Disorder: A Handbook for Diagnosis and Treatment (3rd ed.), by Russell A. Barkley

Attention Deficit Hyperactivity Disorder: Questions & Answers for Parents, by Gregory S. Greenberg and Wade F. Horn

A Comprehensive Guide to Attention Deficit Disorder in Adults, edited by Kathleen G. Nadeau

Driven to Distraction: Recognizing and Coping With Attention Deficit Disorder From Childhood Through Adulthood, by Edward M. Hallowell and John J. Ratey

Dr. Larry Silver's Advice to Parents on ADHD (2nd ed.), by Larry B. Silver

Hyperactive Children Grown Up: ADHD in Children, Adolescents, and Adults (2nd ed.), by Gabrielle Weiss and Lily Trokenberg Hechtman

Keys to Parenting a Child With Attention Deficit Disorders (2nd ed.), by Barry E. McNamara and Francine J. McNamara

Late, Lost, and Unprepared: A Parents' Guide to Helping Children With Executive Functioning, by Joyce Cooper-Kahn and Laurie Dietzel

Mastering Your Adult ADHD: A Cognitive-Behavioral Treatment Program, by Steven A. Safren, Susan Sprich, Carol A. Perlman, & Michael W. Otto

Maybe You Know My Kid: A Parents' Guide to Identifying, Understanding and Helping Your Child With Attention-Deficit Hyperactivity Disorder (3rd ed.), by Mary Fowler

Maybe You Know My Teen: A Parent's Guide to Helping Your Adolescent With Attention Deficit Hyperactivity Disorder, by Mary Fowler

Parenting Children With ADHD: 10 Lessons That Medicine Cannot Teach, by Vincent J. Monastra

Put Yourself in Their Shoes: Understanding Teenagers With Attention Deficit Hyperactivity Disorder, by Harvey C. Parker

School Success for Kids With ADHD, by Stephan M. Silverman, Jacqueline S. Iseman, and Sue Jeweler

Taking Charge of ADHD: The Complete, Authoritative Guide for Parents (Rev. ed.), by Russell A. Barkley

The AD/HD Parenting Handbook: Practical Advice for Parents From Parents, by Colleen Alexander-Roberts

The Misunderstood Child: Understanding and Coping With Your Child's Learning Disabilities (4th ed.), by Larry B. Silver

Understanding Girls With AD/HD, by Kathleen G. Nadeau, Ellen B. Littman, & Patricia O. Quinn

BOOKS FOR STUDENTS

A Bird's-Eye View of Life With ADD and ADHD: Advice From Young Survivors, by Chris A. Zeigler Dendy and Alex Zeigler

ADD and the College Student: A Guide for High School and College Students With Attention Deficit Disorder (Rev. ed.), edited by Patricia O. Quinn

Adolescents and ADD: Gaining the Advantage, by Patricia O. Quinn

ADD-Friendly Ways to Organize Your Life, by Judith Kolberg and Kathleen G. Nadeau

Attention, Girls! A Guide to Learn All About Your AD/HD by Patricia O. Quinn

Coaching College Students With AD/HD: Issues and Answers, by Patricia O. Quinn, Nancy A. Ratey, and Theresa L. Maitland

The Girls' Guide to AD/HD: Don't Lose This Book!, by Beth Walker

I Would if I Could: A Teenager's Guide to ADHD/Hyperactivity by Michael Gordon

Joey Pigza Swallowed the Key by Jack Gantos

Jumpin' Johnny Get Back to Work! A Child's Guide to ADHD/Hyperactivity, by Michael Gordon

Learning to Slow Down and Pay Attention: A Book for Kids About ADHD, by Kathleen G. Nadeau and Ellen B. Dixon

Putting on the Brakes: Young People's Guide to Understanding Attention Deficit Hyperactivity Disorder (Rev. ed.), by Patricia O. Quinn and Judith M. Stern

Shelley, the Hyperactive Turtle, by Deborah M. Moss

Sparky's Excellent Misadventures: My A.D.D Journal, by Phyllis Carpenter and Marti Ford

The Survival Guide for Kids With ADD or ADHD by John F. Taylor

Zipper: The Kid With ADHD, by Caroline Janover

ORGANIZATIONS

Attention Deficit Disorder Association
P.O. Box 7557
Wilmington, DE 19803
(800) 939-1019
info@add.org
http://www.add.org

CHADD (Children and Adults with Attention-Deficit/Hyperactivity Disorder)
8181 Professional Place, Ste. 150
Landover, MD 20785
(301) 306-7070; (800) 233-4050
http://www.chadd.org

Council for Exceptional Children
1110 North Glebe Road, Ste. 300
Arlington, VA 22201
(888) 232-7733
service@cec.sped.org
http://www.cec.sped.org

The International Dyslexia Association
40 York Road, 4th Floor
Baltimore, MD 21204
(410) 296-0232; (800) 222-3123
http://www.interdys.org

Learning Disabilities Association of America
4156 Library Road
Pittsburgh, PA 15234
(412) 341-1515
info@ldaamerica.org
http://www.ldanatl.org

National Center for Learning Disabilities
381 Park Avenue South, Ste. 1401
New York, NY 10016
(212) 545-7510; (888) 575-7373
ncld@ncld.org
http://www.ncld.org

WEBSITES

2e (Twice-Exceptional) Newsletter
http://www.2enewsletter.com

A.D.D. WareHouse
http://www.addwarehouse.com

Attention Deficit Disorder Association
http://www.add.org

The Center: A Resource for Women and Girls With AD/HD
http://www.ncgiadd.org

Children and Adults with Attention-Deficit/Hyperactivity Disorder
http://www.chadd.org

LD OnLine
http://www.ldonline.org

Learning Disabilities Association of America
http://ldanatl.org

Wrightslaw Special Education Law and Advocacy
http://www.wrightslaw.com

REFERENCES

American Psychiatric Association. (1968). *Diagnostic and statistical manual of mental disorders* (2nd ed.). Washington, DC: Author.

American Psychiatric Association. (1980). *Diagnostic and statistical manual of mental disorders* (3rd ed.). Washington, DC: Author.

American Psychiatric Association. (1994). *Diagnostic and statistical manual of mental disorders* (4th ed.). Washington, DC: Author.

American Psychiatric Association. (2000). *Diagnostic and statistical manual* (4th ed., Rev.). Washington, DC: Author.

Americans with Disabilities Act, 42 U.S.C. §§ 12102 et seq. (1990).

Barkley, R. A. (1993). A new theory of ADHD. *ADHD Report, 1*(5), 1–4.

Barkley, R. A. (2006). *Attention Deficit Hyperactivity Disorder.* New York, NY: Guilford.

Barkley, R. (2008). *Advances in ADHD: Theory, diagnosis and management* [DVD]. Lancaster, PA: J&K Seminars.

Barkley, R. A., & Murphy, K. R. (1996). Psychological adjustment and adaptive impairments in young adults with ADHD. *Journal of Attention Disorders, 1,* 41–54.

Barkley, R. A., & Murphy, K. R. (2002). Driving in young adults with Attention Deficit Hyperactivity Disorder: Knowledge, performance, adverse outcomes and role of executive functioning. *Journal of the International Neuropsychological Society, 8,* 655–672.

Barkley, R. A., Murphy, K. R., & Fischer, M. (2008). *ADHD in adults: What the science says.* New York, NY: Guilford.

Bird, H. R., & Gould, M. S. (1993). Patterns of diagnostic comorbidity in a community sample of children aged nine through sixteen years. *Journal of the American Academy of Child and Adolescent Psychiatry, 32,* 361–368.

Brown, T. E. (2005). *Attention Deficit Disorder.* New Haven, CT: Yale University Press.

Denckla, M. B. (1996). A theory and model of executive function. In W. G. Lyon & N. A. Krasnegor (Eds.), *Attention, memory and executive function* (pp. 263–278). Baltimore, MD: Paul H. Brookes.

Gregg, N. (2009). *Adolescents and adults with learning disabilities and ADHD: Assessment and accommodation.* New York, NY: Guilford.

Honos-Webb, L. (2005). *The gift of ADHD.* Oakland, CA: New Harbinger Publications.

Individuals with Disabilities Education Act, 20 U.S.C. 1401 et. seq. (1990).

MTA Cooperative Group. (1999). A fourteen-month randomized clinical trial of treatment strategies for Attention-Deficit/Hyperactivity Disorder. *Archives of General Psychiatry, 56,* 1073–1086.

National Institute of Mental Health. (n.d.). *Attention Deficit Hyperactivity Disorder (ADHD)* [Brochure]. Bethesda, MD: Author.

Nigg, J. T. (2006). *What causes ADHD? Understanding what goes wrong and why.* New York, NY: Guilford.

Parker, H. C. (2002). *Problem solver guide for students with ADHD.* Plantation, FL: Specialty.

Perry, B. D. (1998). Neurophysiological aspects of anxiety disorders in children. In C. E. Coffey & R. A. Brumback (Eds.), *Textbook of pediatric neuropsychiatry* (pp. 579–594). Washington DC: American Psychiatric.

Ratey, J. J., & Hagerman, E. (2008). *Spark: The revolutionary new science of exercise and the brain.* New York, NY: Little, Brown.

Reiff, M. I., & Tippins, S. (Eds.). (2004). *ADHD complete and authoritative guide.* Elk Grove Village, IL: American Academy of Pediatrics.

Rowling, J. K. (1999). *Harry Potter and the chamber of secrets.* New York, NY: Scholastic.

Section 504 of the Rehabilitation Act (1973). 29 U.S.C. Section 706 et. seq.

Shaw, P., Eckstrand, K., Blumenthal, J., Lerch, J. P., Classen, L., Evans, A., ... Rapoport, J. L. (2007). Attention-deficit/hyperactivity disorder is characterized by a delay in cortical maturation. *Proceedings of the National Academy of Sciences, 104*, 19649–19654.

Swanson, H. L., & Saez, L. (2003). Memory difficulties in children and adults with learning disabilities. In H. L. Swanson, K. R. Harris, & S. Graham (Eds.), *Handbook of learning disabilities* (pp. 182–198). New York, NY: Guilford.

Tannock, R., & Brown, T. E. (2000). Attention-Deficit/Hyperactivity Disorder with learning disorders in children and adolescents. In T. E. Brown (Ed.), *Attention-Deficit Disorders and comorbidities in children, adolescents, and adults* (pp. 231–295). Washington, DC: American Psychiatric.

Weiss, G., & Hechtman, L. T. (1986). *Hyperactive children grown up: ADHD in children, adolescents, and adults* (2nd ed.). New York, NY: Guilford.

Wright, P. W., & Wright, P. D. (2007). *Special education law* (2nd ed.). Hartfield, VA: Harbor House Law.

ABOUT THE AUTHORS

Ruth B. Spodak, Ph.D., founding partner of Spodak, Stefano and Associates, has worked in the special education field as a licensed psychologist, educator, counselor, lecturer, author, and advocate for more than 30 years. In 1989, she founded Ruth Spodak & Associates, a private practice specializing in testing, evaluation, and diagnosis of individuals with learning disabilities and Attention Deficit/Hyperactivity Disorder (ADHD). In providing and coordinating intervention services for academic, emotional, and social development, Dr. Spodak counseled students, parents, and teachers for understanding of learning disabilities and development of effective support systems. Before entering private practice, Dr. Spodak worked as director of the schools division at the National Institute of Dyslexia (NID), formerly known as the TRI-Services Center, where she helped establish model training programs and workshops for learning disabled and dyslexic children.

Dr. Spodak organized and directed the Center School, a private school for children with learning disabilities. During her tenure, the school earned an Excellence in Education award from the U.S. Department of Education. Prior to that, she served as Assistant Head of The McLean School, where she was responsible for directing programs addressing students with mild learning difficulties.

Throughout her career, Dr. Spodak has lectured at the university level, authored many articles, and conducted research for Head Start programs. She earned a B.A. in psychology at Brown University and completed her graduate training at the University of Maryland.

Kenneth Stefano, Psy.D, founding partner of Spodak, Stefano and Associates, is a clinical psychologist who has worked with children, adolescents, and families for the last 20 years. After completing his doctoral internship at the John L. Gildner Regional Institute for Children and Adolescents (JLG-RICA), he joined the JLG-RICA staff as a psychologist, remaining for the next 15 years. Dr. Stefano assumed various roles during his tenure at JLG-RICA, including providing intensive individual and family therapy to seriously emotionally disturbed students in a residential setting. Dr. Stefano also served as the staff psychologist on the JLG-RICA Evaluation Unit, administering psychological evaluations to children and adolescents referred by the court system.

From 2004 to 2007, Dr. Stefano served as Clinical Director of the Evaluation Unit, managing a multidisciplinary team of professionals who provided comprehensive diagnostic and placement evaluations for the juvenile court of Montgomery County, MD. Prior to that, he was the Institute's Director of Psychology Internship Training, leading efforts to select, train, and supervise predoctoral psychology students.

In addition to his extensive clinical and assessment experience, Dr. Stefano has provided expert testimony at juvenile court proceedings, as well as advocacy for local public school students with learning and emotional problems. Dr. Stefano graduated from the University of Pittsburgh with a B.S. in psychology/communications and completed his graduate training at Indiana University of Pennsylvania.